T0129757

*From*
# PRODIGAL
*to*
# HELD,
*A Diary of Hurt and Hope*

—— LUCY B. ADAMS ——

**author**HOUSE®

*AuthorHouse™*
*1663 Liberty Drive*
*Bloomington, IN 47403*
*www.authorhouse.com*
*Phone: 1 (800) 839-8640*

*Published by AuthorHouse 4/24/2020*

*ISBN: 978-1-7283-3789-0 (sc)*
*ISBN: 978-1-7283-3759-3 (e)*

*Print information available on the last page.*

*Any people depicted in stock imagery provided by Getty Images are models, and such images are being used for illustrative purposes only. Certain stock imagery © Getty Images.*

*THE HOLY BIBLE, NEW INTERNATIONAL VERSION®, NIV® Copyright © 1973, 1978, 1984, 2011 by Biblica, Inc.® Used by permission. All rights reserved worldwide.*

*This book is printed on acid-free paper.*

This book is dedicated to God, who gave me new life in Him. It is also for His angels on earth who helped me pull myself together through the estrangement of my daughter not once but twice. The hand of God was working specifically through those who walked with me, and continue to walk with me, during this excruciating time. You are inscribed upon my heart, and I am eternally grateful and thankful for each of you, my sisters and brothers in Christ. Without your loving support, cheerleading, prayers, gluten-free junk food, sitting with me while the tears flowed, and all the truth you spoke in love, I would not be the woman I am today. Thank you for walking the walk and talking the talk, and for never making me feel alone.

To my dear friend Lisa and her husband and my former boss, Rodney. "Thank you" does not encompass the feelings I have for you both. From the office talks to beach trips and hard conversations that helped me see my worth, I love you both and am blessed to call you family.

To my sweet friends Diane and Greg. Thanks for always being a part of my life for over twenty years. I love you both, and you have helped me in ways I'll never be able to convey.

To Melanie, who is no longer a part of my life, lived with me and saw the pain of Aurora's first departure, and showed me I can be loved but it had to be by the right person at the right time. Thank you for loving me when I didn't love myself, and for standing by me even though it was painful to you.

To Carol, who has been my friend since 1991 and knows my life and heart better than I do at times. Thank you for all your encouragement, cards, brunches, and conversations. I love you and your family, and your tenacity and humor have sustained me on the hardest of days.

To the DC Chicks, Gary Napier, and the Entire Wednesday Night Table Group. You taught me that God loves us, and we must love ourselves to be able to walk the walk and talk to the talk.

To Kailey Adams. Thank you for being my first editor. Thank you for showing me that single moms can make mistakes and still have their children love and respect them. You are a breath of fresh air every day.

To my parents, Steve and Pam, and my sister, Debbie. Thank you for accepting me back into the family and loving me for who I was, who I am, and who I am becoming. You three mean so much to me, and I love our lives and where God is taking all of us.

To my husband, David. Thank you for picking up my cross and walking with me. Your hugs, smiles, words of wisdom, and never-ending devotion to Christ (and to me) have been my miracle on earth. No one loves and accepts me as you do. Thank you for loving who I am and not dwelling on who I was before I fully understood who Christ is and what He has done for the world. I am forgiven and chosen, and you remind of that, especially on the hard days. You were a great stepfather, father-in-law, and papa who loved unconditionally and spoke truth in love.

---

> You are those who have stood by me in my trials.
> (Luke 22:28)

---

And to my daughter, Aurora, who chose to walk away because I was not who you needed or wanted, and who had to endure the down times of my life. I love you more than you could ever imagine. You once told me that as a mom, you cannot believe I would write a book that "makes her child look like a monster." My precious, precious child, if you ever read this book, you will see this book is not about you at all. It's about your mother finding her way back to life, and it was in your leaving the first time that I was able to find myself and seek my way back to the God who loves me. You once took me outside, spread a blanket on the ground, and told me to look at the stars and remember if God can take care of those stars in the sky, He would take care of me. That moment of love is forever engraved on my heart. It's one of those rare moments I remember you loved me.

I cannot express how incredibly sorry for all the pain my life has caused you, and as you age and raise your children, you will find all parents make mistakes, and all parents do things in life that hurt their children's feelings, but they are not done with malice or intent. Parents do the best they can at the time and love unconditionally, as I did, and I will always love you unconditionally. Grumpiness on parents' part does not mean we don't love our children. As I apologized to you many times for my grumpy or angry moments, I hope you someday remember the happy moments we shared … As your father abandoned you, his father abandoned him, and as you abandoned me, I hope your children break the cycle of estrangement. I never want you to feel the broken heart of a mother being childless. I love you, Aurora. You always have been and always will be my hero. I long to hear your voice, see your smile, and hug you. I will always be waiting for you to come home.

To my grandchildren, Owen and Katherine. I hope someday you will know your Mimsey, her heart, and all her mistakes that made her stronger and full of hope for her entire family to be united. You are loved and adored.

The key is to have a forgiving spirit and realize all people, even parents, are human.

# Contents

# *Prologue*

The story I am about to tell is not intended to shame or hurt anyone involved. It's my story, my truth. It's my path to becoming the prodigal daughter who eventually, through trials and heartache, returned to my heavenly Father to be chosen and held. In turn, I long for my own daughter to return to me. During the writing of this diary, I had no one to lean on, really, who had experienced exactly what I was going through. However, I learned through the second season of my storm that other parents also had children who had turned their backs and walked away without so much as a goodbye. It's incredibly heartbreaking when all communication is exterminated from the one to whom you give birth. I never claimed to be the perfect parent, or the perfect daughter for my own parents. Parenthood doesn't come with an instruction manual, and all parents do the best we can.

What I've learned through lots of therapy is that everyone—yes, every single person who walks the planet we call home—enters adulthood with scars from childhood. What bothers us about our childhood leads to overcompensating during adulthood and through our own parenting. Being the parent we needed to our own children is probably not what they need and therefore can lead to estrangement.

I lost my earthly family through the first estrangement, but I learned so much about myself because I allowed myself to think and feel on my own. There was no pressure from anyone to tell me how I felt or what to think about situations. In a sense, the first estrangement was a story of hope for my family to reconcile and be a whole family. We must renew our spirit when we have given up. We must pursue courage to continue to wake up every morning and shed the covers when we want to snuggle down into the shame we feel. I am very thankful and grateful to those listed on the dedication page of this book; they kept me going and wouldn't let me give up! They encouraged me to find myself first and find my way back to God, and eventually they believed my daughter would find her way home, and our relationship would be reconciled.

When I first thought about publishing this book, it was after my daughter had called after an estrangement of one year, three months, nineteen days, and five hours. I can remember sitting in our home office and seeing my daughter's boyfriend's number pop up on my phone. My husband was at Bible study, and I couldn't answer. I called him and told him "Luke" was calling, and he immediately came home from Bible study. We answered the phone together, and it was pure heaven to me. I kept crying and telling her, "I cannot change the past, and I'm sorry for how I hurt you, but I can make our future better." I asked why she had decided to call me after all this time, and she said she had read my blog (the bulk of this book). In her reading, she felt I had changed and wanted to give our relationship a try again. We agreed to meet for coffee and seeing her face after all that time was pure joy for me.

However, all good things must come to an end, and unfortunately, after just shy of two years, my daughter again told me she did not want me to be a part of her life. The book I was writing made her "look like a monster," and she could not believe any mother would present her child in this way. Now that her son was getting older, she didn't want me to speak ill of her and "turn her child against her." To her, my Christianity was a lie, my marriage was a lie, and my entire being was a lie. She stated unless I came clean and told everyone the truth about our lives, she could no longer be a part of my life. So I did just that. I made a post on Facebook, which is the most public forum I can think of, and stated that everything that had transpired between her and me was completely my fault. I was a horrible mother and a horrible person, and I asked everyone to forgive me for being such a worthless piece of human flesh. That public statement did not change a thing, and now it was been exactly one year, eight months, five days, and twenty-three hours to the day since I have seen or talked to her.

So how does estrangement from a child affect a mother's psyche? For me, I called a psychologist and took every test available to see what kind of mental illness I must be suffering from. I was tested for bipolar disorder, multiple personality disorder, narcissism, and schizophrenia. The conclusion? I am suffering from severe depression. I could have answered that question without spending five hundred dollars a pop (I took these tests four times), but that's okay. Now I have released myself from being mentally ill, but that begs the question, "If you are not mentally ill, why did your daughter leave? What abuse did you bestow upon her to make her leave?" These are questions I have continuously asked myself for the past five years.

If you are reading this book, I am guessing you are in a similar situation. Let me start by saying I am extremely sorry for your estrangement, and I hope my journey brings a little bit of peace as you start your own journey of hope of reconciliation, or you began to release yourself from what seems to be a trend of children today to accuse, attack, and then to cut all ties from the people who want the best for them and would walk through fire to have them back.

## *Background*

I guess I should start with my own childhood. I grew up in the shadow of perfection (or so I thought), a sister with perfectly straight teeth and a head full of hair like Julia Roberts. She was petite with fair skin and dark hair, and she was everyone's dream child. Quiet. Girlie. Didn't make messes. My parents often tease the doctor could hear me crying before I even popped out! I wouldn't eat anything but bananas for the first two years of life, and I had naturally straight hair and a mouth full of wire at sixteen, not to mention I was taller and chunkier than my sister.

I do not, nor did I ever, begrudge my sister her perfection. I wanted to be her many times. My failings are not her fault, and I've never blamed her for my shortcomings; I was who God made me. Where she was calm, I had a temper, felt misunderstood, and didn't really know how to convey my thoughts and feelings. My own faults and self-doubt led to an eating disorder that started when I was sixteen and followed me well into my thirties.

I accepted Christ into my heart when I was ten and twenty, but I'm not sure I did it for all the right reasons. Maybe at the time, I knew Christ was my savior and wanted to follow Him, and I believe Christ recognized my heart at the time. All my life, I read my Bible, taught Sunday school, and helped lead a children's choir. I read Christian books written by Christian authors and truly believed I was doing all God wanted me to do. Me and God. God and Me. This was something I thought daily. We were one, me and Him.

In 1995, I delivered via C-section a beautiful baby girl. She was and always has been the joy of my life. She could make me smile by her presence, her smile, and her funny way of saying words like "tefealone" for telephone, or "culculator" for calculator. Every summer after junior high, we would watch the entire ten seasons of the show *Friends*. We loved to watch musicals like *Chicago*, *Mamma Mia*, and *Rent*, as well as Disney movies. One of our favorite nights was movies and Krispy Kreme donut runs in our pajamas. She could devour two or three donuts before we got home with the dozen, and I would often tease her as she ate them. The look on her face would make me chuckle, and we would listen to music while I drove and she devoured.

It wasn't always fun and games like when she received a cancer diagnosis. She was diagnosed with leukemia just after Christmas of her third year on earth. Thankfully, she survived, and the whole cancer experience changed my life in one way. It made me even more thankful for her life, and her perspective on life always amazed me. During this time, I became her biggest cheerleader and an advocate for the Leukemia and Lymphoma Society. Five years after her diagnosis, I divorced her father, which changed my life in good and bad ways. But nothing, and I do mean nothing, we experienced could have prepared me for when she (in my words) ran away. In her words, "I left because of a difficult roommate you had, and her daughters who were driving me crazy." I consider it running away because for one year, three months, nineteen days, and five hours, there was absolutely no communication between her and me. I had "message takers," but nothing about her life was ever conveyed back to me. (I've since learned the silence from family members who see your child on a regular basis contributes to isolation of the estranged parent.)

At the time, did I see this as a "God thing" and as an opportunity to take me away from some sin patterns in my life? Nope. But now, looking back, I see where God was heavily at work in my life to give me the love I had always dreamed of, both in friends, in family, and in a husband.

Again, I reiterate, this book is not intended to make anyone feel bad about their parenting skills or their sin patterns. It is about me, really—how I ended up there and arrived here. I guess this is also a source of contention for my daughter, because it is talking about me, which conveys narcissism. And I can accept that. We are allowed to share our feelings, no matter who we are. We share what God gives and takes away, and it is how we handle our suffering and blessings that matters. It is about hope and faith, and my intention is to help parents who have an estranged child or who discover they themselves may be the prodigal child.

Of course, I never saw myself as prodigal. But when I took a great look at myself, I realized I was making decisions and living a life that could have made my daughter feel less than important. You'll find through the reading of this diary it was never intentional or with malice toward her, and I am forever regretful of some decisions. I also realize I had put a tremendous amount of pressure on myself as a single mom to make sure every decision I made was right, correct, and thought through. As I strove to be perfect, I was failing and would mentally beat myself up with every waking moment. To say I felt a weight of the sinking *Titanic* in my chest moment to moment would not come close to how I felt, but I kept going because I felt I didn't have a choice. I looked to the wrong anchors to save me. I needed Christ, and I needed Him fast and now, or my life would continue to spiral like the tornado that had already caused damage.

# December 18, 2014—The Loss of a Child

Do not be far from me, because distress is near and there is no one to help. (Psalm 22:11 NIV)

How do you learn to deal with a situation out of your control? No, my daughter didn't die; she ran away. The day she did, I died a little. She has been gone for thirty-four days now, and I'm about ready to lose my mind. From my perspective, and like I told her, she overreacted big time to what I believed would be a good solution to what I thought she wanted. In the few weeks before she left, she was moody and grumpy and seemed tired a lot. I hadn't seen her for more than thirty minutes in the three weeks before she left. She even said, "Yes, my boyfriend says I'm that way too."

I said, "Maybe you should stay home and rest some, and not run the highway so much." Isn't that what a good mom would say? The week she left, several little events happened, but nothing out of the ordinary mother-daughter realm. She asked someone I used to know to buy her shoes I was going to buy her, but I wanted to make is a surprise. In hindsight, I now realize I should have seen the warning signs, but I didn't. Now I regret having health issues and work issues and life in general, but so life goes.

In the weeks before she left, we had a few discussions, but nothing I would call fights. I did talk to her about Thanksgiving weekend and how hurt I was that she spent an hour with me for Thanksgiving, missed out on an opportunity to get someone I used to know a birthday present, and then ditched me for the annual putting up the Christmas tree on a Sunday afternoon. When I did speak to her about this, I prefaced the statement with, "I am about to tell you some things you probably don't want to hear, but I need to get it off my chest." She didn't seem particularly upset by what I said and promptly said she was sorry. I even asked someone else about these events and whether I, as a parent, was out of line for the way I felt. In no way did I yell or scream; I calmly told her how I felt. I was told, "Yes, you were fine with how you felt." Little did I know this person would soon turn on me.

The next event when I should have realized my daughter was not right was the shopping for a dress. I took her shopping for a dress for her to wear to a special event, and she needed shoes to go with it. I told her to look at the shoes she had at home, and we would see what would work and whether we needed to get a pair. During this dress shopping trip, I purchased two hundred dollars' worth of clothes for her, and boy, did I enjoy this short shopping spree. Since the arrival of the boyfriend, college, and her work schedule, I felt as if I really hadn't seen much of her.

Another warning sign was because she did work and I never see her due to our conflicting schedules, I thought about taking her to breakfast. When the day before our breakfast date came, I didn't have the money to go, so I canceled breakfast but told her to let me know when her break was, and I would bring her lunch. The call never came. What a whirlwind she was when she came home from work that night, grabbed something, and then left. She later told me I could have come by her work anytime and eaten lunch. I didn't know this, or I would have!

When the Monday before the "dress event came, I got a call from her at work, and she asked if she could use my credit card to go shopping for shoes. I told her I would think about it. To my surprise, she found someone else to take her shoe shopping, robbing me of my joy of taking her shopping again. To be able to purchase the shoes for my child, I called the person who took her shopping and asked to reimburse them for my child's shoes. "No," this person said, "she didn't ask me to purchase the shoes, but still I wanted to pay for them." Then came a half-hour talk about how hard it is for an adult to live in another adult's house, and how maybe I should come up with a contract for her. *Blah, blah, blah,* I thought. *Since when do my child and I have trouble communicating?*

Then came the little talk after that about "Please, child, do not put me in that position where I have to listen to someone else tell me how to raise you. Or, don't humiliate me by acting like I'm not going to provide for you what I know you need. If I can't afford to get you shoes, I'll ask for help. But, dear child, you robbed me of spending time with you! Please don't do it again." During this conversation, I also brought up the boyfriend, whom I hadn't seen since November 25 when I asked him not to lie on the couch with my daughter. He promptly asked me why I had a problem with that, and I said, "Because for two people who wish to remain pure until marriage, you are playing with fire." I guess he really didn't like my explanation, but I wouldn't care how old two people are and whether they were married or single—I do not want to see anyone lying on the couch together. For a "gentleman" who told me upon first meeting me that he feels it is inappropriate to enter a girl's room, this certainly seems odd that he would be disrespectful of how I felt about this. And that's the last conversation I ever had with him! The excuse for him not ever coming around was car trouble, the rebuilding another car, and his parents loaning him a car that "wasn't reliable." Like a fool, I believed all this.

The Tuesday before she left, I had a conversation while at an exercise class with a "friend." I told her how I was wondering whether I was an unreasonable parent for wanting my child to do a few dishes a day, feed one dog, let the dogs out and back in before she left for work, and change out the laundry every now and again. Was I wrong for my feelings about Thanksgiving weekend? Was I doing something wrong as a parent? This person agreed with me: "If she wants to be an adult, you have to show her how to do things, and who does she think has been cleaning up her messes for twenty years?"

I thought to myself, *I can most certainly approach her tonight and have a different feel for what to say and how to approach her wanting to move out and not being responsible for any messes.*

You have to understand that in the last two years of her high school career, I worked three jobs at times to make ends meet so she could enjoy her high school friends and activities and concentrate on schooling so she could maybe enter college with her freshman year behind her. However, in her senior year, she was working, so with the help of a friend, I decided to get her a car! See, my child was working steady and had several different irons in the fire, and I felt maybe a car with low miles, and a low $240 payment for car, car insurance, and phone all rolled into one, would teach her responsibility and give her freedom from having Mommy take her everywhere.

Well, I was told the day before she left that she didn't really want all I had done. She didn't want the car and didn't want the $240 car payment because it took all her money, and she "didn't ever get to have fun." She didn't want to "clean up other people's messes." (I didn't know plates, cups, and a fork or two was too much for a college kid to do. A warning, parents: don't ask them to do dishes.) So like a mother will do, I explained to her that if she tried to get her own apartment, she would need rent money, utility money, health insurance, car insurance, appliances, furniture, and money for food. She may have to get a second job to afford all this, and then where would school be? What was wrong with living at home where she had free room and board, a fridge full of food, meals cooked and left on plates in the fridge, a laundry room, and all the free TV a kid could want? The bonus was the house was hers and hers alone from 7:15 every morning until 5:30 every night. That was a jackpot, if you ask me. I said, "I know it isn't easy living with someone else, but we can make it work. If you and your boyfriend want to come here for dinner instead of you driving to his house every day and losing forty-five minutes each way, I'll pay for him to come here. I'll cook meals." I said so many things that I keep wondering whether I should regret them.

Should I regret explaining how much the cost of living is? Should I regret speaking to people who would come to turn their backs on me once she left? Should I regret telling her boyfriend I don't want him lying on the couch with my daughter? Should I regret telling someone I was going to buy her the shoes and was frustrated with her attitude? (Yes, to this one.) Should I regret telling her I would check into dorm living, and maybe she could live there? Should I regret telling her how much she hurt my feelings over Thanksgiving?

Do I regret calling the school, checking into the dorms, and telling her we could check into that but it may cost her more if scholarships don't pay? Yes. I think she was thinking that was what I wanted her to do, so she ran. I didn't know she was going to do that. I thought I was going to bring the paperwork home on that Friday night, and we would watch *Friends* and eat junk food for celiacs and talk about what she really wanted. That was not what so-called friends were telling me she wanted because obviously they know her better than I do. A half hour before work was over, I texted her to find out what she may want for carry out, and her return to me was, "Thanks, but I think I'll figure something out tonight. Cat and I have found somewhere else to live." Her next message was, "It's fine, I'm safe."

"Really?" I said. "That's what you want to say to me? I think you overreacted, and I'm tired of people telling me what you want. I guess you are not speaking to me. I called the police, so expect a call. I hope you know what you're doing. What shall I do with your car?" By this time, I had made it home, saw her car in the driveway, and wasn't panicked. I came into the house and yelled her name while running into her room, which was devoid of clothes and knickknacks, but she left anything I had ever given her. I again called some people I knew, and they very calmly told me to calm down. Seriously? How in the world do you stay calm when you child is gone?

The police came and asked everything a mom always wants to hear. "Did you have a fight?" No. "Is she on drugs?" No. "Is she with her boyfriend?" I don't know. "Do you approve of him?" How would I know? I barely know him. "Well, ma'am, because she is nineteen, we really can't do anything. You'll just have to wait for her to call you and for her to talk to you." What you aren't understanding, Officer Fat Belly, is that my child and I do not have problems. We don't fight. I would come to say that very sentence a thousand times over thirty-four days.

I then thought about her bank account and how it barely had any money in it. While at the bank, she walked in, smiling and waving to the teller, and as soon as she saw me, her face went blank. I turned and said, "What are you doing?"

Her boyfriend promptly said, "You didn't give her a choice."

I looked at him, raised my hand, and said, "You had best not speak to me right now."

With a smile on his face, he said, "That's no problem."

I looked at my beautiful child, and my life flashed before my eyes. "Yes, you did have a choice. You could have waited for me to come home, and we could have talked about this. But you chose to do this instead."

"Yep," she said, so cold and unlike the child I'd raised. I wonder where this hatred and attitude is coming from. Doesn't she know I love her and only want what's best for her? That would be the last time I would see, hug, or hear from her. It's now been thirty-four days.

I called the people I used to know and explained the situation to them, but after receiving what I will call a lecture, I said three times that I need to hang up, and I did, I needed to be alone in my thoughts and my sorrow.

You know, you really find out how much people truly think of you, how well they know you, and how much they will support you in a situation like this. These people who I thought were my support, who I thought understood and appreciated all I have done and sacrificed for my child, who I thought believed I would do anything for and would die before I would let anyone hurt her, have turned on me faster than lightning strikes. For thirty-three days, I had no understanding of why. Now I do. You see, this precious child whom I would still take a bullet for and still love to the end of the earth, has made it so I have trouble breathing. What's a mom to do? I went for twenty days calling hospitals and checking obits to see if she was alive or dead because I didn't know. Kids are smart these days. They can suspend their own phones, block you from all forms of social media, and have their friends block you so you cannot get hold of anyone. Then, people who you think know you tell you that because you hid things from your past from them (these things are painful events that I do not like to talk about), they cannot believe a word you say, and they have to believe what your child has said. Then they shut you out too, all the while admitting they have known where your child was all this time. They even helped her move out and are housing her, and then they get mad at you for pointing out that this could have been handled differently. They don't want to hear that you want your child back, need her, and want to help her with whatever is going on.

What I do know is that my child is emotionally wounded, and I cannot get to her. What I do know is every night, I go to sleep knowing I just faced twenty-four hours without her, and I will wake up tomorrow not knowing if this is another day I'll have to face without her. What I do know is that I have the love and support of my church, friends, neighbors, and employer, but all that pales to the love I had from my child. What I do know is that every day, my heart breaks just a little bit more, and I sleep with her blanket, wear her class ring, and pray and beg God to bring her home. What I do know is for the past thirty-four days, I have wept, prayed, wept, prayed, and clung to my friend while crying out, "Where is she? I want her back. Why doesn't she love me? Why is she doing this?" over and over and over again.

My thoughts frequently turn to, What if she dies? How will I know if she is sick or injured? What if I die? What if I get sick? Will she know? Will she care? Would she come to my funeral? Will I ever see her face? Will I ever get to hug her again? Why doesn't she call? Why doesn't she write? I've sent four cards; are the people she is living with giving her these items? Did she read how I got the tattoo of a cross and butterfly, the cross for Jesus and the butterfly for her? What is she thinking? What is she feeling? It's been thirty-four days, and I'm out of ideas of how to reach out to her. Does she care that my heart is completely broken? Does she know I would do anything to find out what I can do to make it better?

It doesn't help when people say this is normal and every parent goes through this. My parents didn't. I didn't leave them. I didn't keep them from knowing where I was and what I was doing. I just don't understand. I would never want to hurt my family like this. I know they don't feel the same, but that's beside the point. My child is gone. My heart is gone. My world has stopped turning. Each day is like the one before. I get up, I pray, I read a gospel. I shower, go to work, come home, sit and stare at the walls, and wonder where she is. How is she? Does she know I love her? Does she still have a mustard seed of love for me? My life will never be the same. My heart will never be the same. How does a parent deal with missing kids? When they die, you have closure; you at least have a place to visit and talk. When they are just gone, there is no closure, no ending, no reasoning. I try to put my mind somewhere else, but maybe it's just too soon. What does a mother do? We carry our children, nurture our children, and hurt when they hurt. When a child goes missing, everyone blames the mom: "What did you do? Where did you go wrong? Search your heart and find out what you did. Let God guide you in your mistakes."

I have done all that. I have searched, admitted my wrongdoing, and repented to God, to friends, and to my church family. But still this question remains …

Where is my child? My world has changed, and it will never, ever be the same.

---

Here is the world, beautiful and terrible. Things will happen. Do not be afraid. —Frederick Buechner

---

## *January 24, 2015—Broken*

You know how you hear a song when driving in your car, and the lyrics hit you like a ton of bricks? That's totally how I feel about the song "Broken Together" by Casting Crowns. Yes, I know this song is about a married couple who are trying to reconnect and reconcile, but it truly speaks to my heart and can be used in so many situations. The lyrics are as follows.

> What do you think when you look at me, I know we are not the fairy tale you dreamed we'd be … How I wish we could go back to simpler times, before our scars and all our secrets were in the light …

I feel this song so strongly. I have been incredibly broken so many times in my life, and I know—yes, I know—I am not the only one. Like me, many people suffer child abuse, bullying (yes, I was a fat, four-eyed, poodle-haired, crooked-legged mess, but it doesn't mean I deserved the bullying), a broken first marriage, a child's cancer diagnosis, my own cancer diagnosis, a divorce, life as a single mom, a second marriage, a second divorce, and last but not least the loss of a child. How many times can a person find her heart broken and still be able to piece it together? Because I was raised to always think about what the neighbors would think, I sometimes feel (and my therapist would agree) I take on the role of being compassionate to everyone. I take on not only my guilt but everyone's guilt around me. It's a wonder I haven't been completely swallowed by the brokenness

I feel, but I won't and can't give in, because I have God and God has me. Every time I feel I am giving up, I have people, real people, who pick me up and continuously remind me in their own special ways "I am loved".

The saying is correct: God places the right people in your life at exactly the right time. Without these people showing me God's true love through their actions and words, I may be completely broken.

Maybe the song is right: we are not made to be complete. None of us are complete on our own; it takes God working in us, and through the people we surround ourselves with, to truly heal our hearts, heal our minds, and take away our pain. I wish I could hold my child right now and tell her I understand her brokenness. Her childhood was taken away by disease, although I always thought we made the best of the situation, such as her father canceling her tenth birthday and telling her to call him when she grew up, and the years of me telling her he loved her in his own way. I am sure my second failed marriage broke her, and her longing for a true, close girlfriend was shattered by teens who were immature. She had a fear of being abandoned because of so many friends coming and going in her life: her favorite male teacher and father figure she adopted leaving her school, a first boyfriend who had a criminal past (unknown to us)—all these things I feel broke her, and she built a wall around herself, not really hearing me say she needed help or counseling. Maybe I wasn't the best single parent I could have been. Maybe the current feeling of broken she is putting me though isn't about me at all, but about her brokenness.

Does she realize all those thoughts I am having break me again? As parents, we do not want our kids to be broken. We do not want them to ever feel pain. I am not a perfect parent; this I know. I was not the perfect daughter (if my parents could, they would tell you), I was not the perfect sister (she would also gladly tell you), and I am not always the perfect friend and coworker. I am not the perfect neighbor, I am not the perfect employee, I am not the perfect ex-spouse, and I will not be the perfect spouse ever. I am broken, I am not complete.

Am I angry with God for my brokenness? No.

Do I know He has each and every single piece of my brokenness? Yes.

Maybe what truly binds us together as humans is we are all broken. We all have our own story, our pasts, our hurts, our shattered hopes, dreams, and pieces of our life that are incomplete. But my eye turns to God when I am feeling most shattered. My heart turns to His hands to hold the pieces and care for them when I can't. My voice sings to the heavens, asking for healing. Would I truly go back to a time when life was simpler, when I didn't know I was broken? No. The broken pieces of my life have brought me to the place I am now. I stand in God's light, and I am surrounded by people who truly care and love me and feel the pieces of my brokenness with me. Each one of these hurts is a piece my past, a piece of my hurt, a piece of my failure, a piece of my guilt, a piece of my lost loves, a piece of my lost innocence, a piece of my shame, a piece of my puzzle. And when I stand in God's presence, He puts these pieces together, and I am not broken—I am complete.

> Be anxious for nothing, but in everything by prayer and supplication with thanksgiving let your requests be made known to God. And the peace of God, which surpasses all comprehension, will guard your hearts and your minds in Christ Jesus. (Philippians 4:6–7 NIV)

# *January 27, 2015—Missing the Missing*

Today is an important mother-daughter day. Today, Aurora would celebrate sixteen years of remission. I'm incredibly sad she is not here to celebrate, but I did send her favorite flower (carnations) to the place where I last know she was staying. I hope she is still there. If not, will the people send them to her, or call her and let her know they are there? It seems like an even harder day because as a mom, you truly remember moments of your child's life: the day you found out you were pregnant, the day you gave birth, the first day home, the first scrape or bump, the first illness (ours just happened to be cancer), the first broken heart, the first award, the first time your child left your house. I certainly wish my memory of the last would be happier. There are so many things I miss right now: her smile, her laugh, her wit, her love of junk food, the way she would pull out of the driveway in her car, watching silly TV shows, the funny things she would say, the way when she said something totally outlandish, she would lean her forehead toward me, and I would playfully smack it.

I miss the way she would come in the bathroom while I showered and sit on the sink and talk, talk, talk. Sometimes she'd talk about important things, and sometimes she'd rattle on about nothing in particular, just catching up. But it was all time spent together.

I miss going for our pajama runs for ice cream or donuts, and the way she would eat her entire portion of whatever before we even got home.

I miss Saturday mornings, when she would crawl in bed with me, and we would lie there and either talk or watch something, just being together.

I miss listening to her sing in the car, reading her school papers, texting her in the morning, her calling me with that "hey" she has, and knowing she had just woken up but was trying to act like she had been awake for a while.

I miss her texting me, "Uh, I need a towel," when she forgot to grab one before she got in the shower.

I miss her runs to Burger King to get a Flamethrower at 9:30 at night.

I miss looking in on her in the middle of the night and seeing her fast asleep and in the starfish position she always slept in.

I miss her cat.

I miss her texts because she is bored. Her funny Facebook posts. Her snide comments about everything in general. I miss her friends.

I miss singing in church with her and knowing we were worshiping together because we have been doing that for nineteen years together, and the way we would look at each other when one of our favorite songs would come on.

So many things I miss, and so many things I am afraid I will miss. I am so afraid I will miss her graduating college, getting engaged, getting married, having her first baby, getting her first house … I am afraid I will die before I ever see her again.

I miss her so much, and as each sun rises and sets, I know we are losing such precious time together. As a Christian, I can rely on God and believe I will see her, but the human element of me, well, that part is scared. And sad. And heartbroken. And childless.

I wonder if she remembers any of the memories I am holding so close to my heart. I wonder if she is okay, if she is eating healthy, exercising, writing her papers, attending school, and working. Does anyone know what today is and what it means to her and me?

Mainly, I wonder, Does she miss me?

Maybe she does miss me, and maybe she doesn't. It'll always be a mystery, and she has never really told me. But it was during this time that my church started a sermon series called Freeway by Mike Foster and Garry Poole. It changed my perspective and my life in ways I may not be able to explain. It mainly freed me from my own chains of sin and taught me how to forgive myself and move closer to Christ.

---

Trust in the Lord with ALL your heart. Lean not on your own understanding, in all your ways submit to him, and he will make your paths straight. (Proverbs 3:5–6)

---

There were days during this time that I didn't think I would get up. Fortunately, I had a great boss who would tell me, "Things are tough, but you have to wake up each day and pull yourself together and come to work. Just sit and cry if you have too, but you have to keep going. You have to keep with your normal routine, whatever that is. Just keep praying and know we have you. But more important, God has you." And He most certainly did.

# January 31, 2015—Answered Prayers, Listening, and Forgiveness

"It'll clear the bitterness away it can even set a prisoner free ... forgiveness." —Matthew West, "Forgiveness"

You know how sometimes people really hurt your feelings, and you have a choice? You can let them in and let them ask for forgiveness, or you can bottle it up and continue to be angry. Well, I definitely fall in the first category. I'm a "Let me tell you what's on my mind" kind of gal, and "Let's work it out." However, I tend to surround myself with the latter. I also carry guilt. Yes, I am a guilt carrier. I feel guilty for each and every bad thing that ever happened in my life or anyone else's. I know why I do these things; I was raised this way. I was raised to always think about what the neighbors would think or any other person I don't know who would think about what I am doing or not doing. I don't remember any member of my immediate family ever apologizing to me for anything. To be honest, I am not allowed to tell anyone in my family anything they have ever done to hurt me because frankly, they do not want to hear it. I understand why: it's hard to admit you have done something that might have hurt someone, and the truth hurts. Sometimes the truth hurts so bad, you feel it from the top of your head to the pit of your stomach. But truth, when spoken in love, can do one of two things. It can help you see an aspect of yourself that could potentially harm you or others, giving you an opportunity to rectify a situation. Or it can hurt you so bad, you do nothing. And when someone tells you, "You hurt me," I truly believe you should apologize, ask for forgiveness, and reconcile the relationship.

I like to think of myself as a very forgiving person. I have forgiven the abuser for the child abuse I suffered. I forgave my first ex-husband for the abuse I suffered at his hands and by his word. I have forgiven past coworkers and friends for what I believed to be harmful situations from them, most times without people even knowing I was hurt.

I recently saw my missing daughter, and, yes, I have forgiven her for leaving me. I forgave her the night she left. As I sat and listened to what she had to say the other night, I have to tell you, I was completely blown away. I had no idea she felt the way she felt about things, and I must say, yes, I was hurt by some things she said. I also believe I now have a few things to work on myself, because if she is hurt, and it's because of something I said or did, I want her forgiveness, and I want to reconcile our relationship.

Seeing her was an answered prayer. I prayed she would call, I prayed she would answer an e-mail, and every Sunday as I sat in church, I prayed I would look up, and there she would be, standing next to me. None of that happened, and I found her purely by God's intervention.

You see, I was at my Wednesday night table group Bible study, and I wanted to see her at her college-age ministry. I asked a minister to go with me. We walked over, and I peeked my head around and didn't see her, which brought me to tears. As I turned to walk away, he gave me a huge hug and said a prayer for us. I then went to my car and decided to get a coffee. I was extremely excited to see her beautiful face the coffee shop window, and I have to say I couldn't wait to walk in, give her a huge hug, and tell her I love her.

I could tell, however, by the look on her face she was not thrilled to see me and truly didn't want to see me. That in and of itself hurt me. Then she, or maybe it was her boyfriend, proceeded to text the man she was staying with, and he promptly showed up without a "Hello, how are you? Good to see you." Nothing. This didn't surprise me, however, because he is one of those people who will never admit he could have wronged anyone. At least, he has never admitted that to me. It's been forty-six years, and I would think an "I'm sorry" would be in there somewhere, but I guess not. And yes, I forgive him too, but I am not in the place where I can forget the hurt I feel he has imposed. I'm sure it will come in time. But that is not the relationship I am worried about or want to concentrate on.

I listened to my child and the pain she feels, and I asked for her forgiveness. I also reiterated, "I love you, and I miss you. I would never do anything to intentionally hurt you." I told her how she is my entire heart.

Matthew West has a song about forgiveness. He talks about how forgiveness is the hardest thing to give away, and that it goes to those who don't deserve it. I believe this is true in some cases but not in others. It's the opposite of how we feel when the pain they caused is just too real. I totally believe this to be true. Does it take everything in me, however, to say the words? No, not when it comes to my daughter.

I've thought about how I would react to seeing her for the first time, what she would say, and what I would say. I envisioned being able to wrap my arms around her and say, "I love you, I've missed you," and her saying, "I love you too, Mom." But that didn't happen. Instead I got an "I'm not ready for that yet" and "If you do *xyz*, I will consider having a relationship with you again." Wow, talk about something that really, truly hurt. As a mother who looks at herself as a pretty good mom, I was deeply wounded.

I was also told a few other things she believes to be true, and I asked forgiveness for those. I will take those words to heart and change those aspects about myself. Do I feel they are totally true? No. I believe she heard part of what I had said at times, and in her teenaged mind, that's how she interpreted it. Will I always validate her feelings and try harder? Yes. To me, part of communicating and listening and forgiving is validating and truly hearing someone. When people are telling you how they feel, you do not interrupt them or tell them they are wrong; you listen to their truth in love.

What hurt the most was when she told me the past four years, to her, have been "all for show." Seriously? You want me to believe all the times you crawled into bed so we could watch TV together, the ice cream and donut runs, the hugs, the sitting on the vanity and talking to me, the crying on my shoulder, the time at the beach, the unsolicited hugs, the times you have said to someone, "My mom is really cool"—those were all lies? You never meant you love me? You never wanted to spend time with me? You never wanted to watch TV and be quiet? The four days at the beach and the car ride listening to Christian music was all a lie? The times you hugged me in church and told the head of my Sunday school department, "My mom is great with kids," was a lie?

All these moments were so special to me. I cannot fake my love for my child. I cannot fake my feelings, the smiles, the hugs full of love. I am not built that way. But if that is the way you feel, I will take you for your word and work through the pain I feel at basically being told you don't love me, and I will move forward. And I forgive you because I do not want to feel any bitterness toward you. Forgiving you sets me free of being held a prisoner of my own feelings.

It's very hard for me to see our lives through her eyes at times, however, and maybe that's because I've been a single mom for so long and had to be mom, dad, and friend. Maybe at times I've made her feel she had to be those things to me.

Was it intentional? No.

Have I already asked God for His forgiveness? Yes.

Do I want her forgiveness? Yes.

Did I ask her to forgive me? Yes.

Do I feel forgiven yet? By God, yes; He truly sees my heart and always have. By her? Not yet, but I know in time it will come. At least, I hope it does.

I think the hardest part of forgiveness is forgiving yourself. These past forty days, I have beaten myself up one side and down the other. I have been made to feel like I am worthless, a bad mom, and an evil person. I have been shunned, blocked out, and given stipulations from my family on what I need to do for them to be in my life. I have not been asked my side of the story. I have not been given an explanation about what is wrong with my child and why she is so upset. I have been told to leave my family alone. I have been screamed at, cussed at, and told I am unappreciative for what they are doing to "protect my child" and "keep her off the street." And before all that, I was told, "I don't want to be involved." Wow. Then I learned the story of the weeks before my child left, things were grossly exaggerated and not entirely true. And instead of anyone coming to me and saying, "Hey, can we talk?" I was simply shut out. I am sure my family feels they are doing what's right, and I am sure they believe in their hearts I am this evil, terrible person because I hid child abuse, other abusive situations, and a few other very painful parts of my life. But that does not make me a bad. What I did was protect myself from being hurt again. It's amazing to me that a counselor, three ministers, friends, neighbors, my boss, my coworkers, and church people can look at me and tell me what I have done to protect myself and things I have said to my child are all normal. I am normal. I am well rounded, I am an honest parent, I am a good parent, I am a strong parent, and I am a strong Christian. I am seeking God's heart every day. I always have.

For those who say they never struggle, for those who say they never wrong anyone, and for those who say they do not need to ask for anyone's forgiveness or are unwilling to offer forgiveness, I feel pity for them. I know I love the unlovable, I know I have tried to reach the unreachable, and I know I ask for help every day in doing the impossible. It's all because I have God in my head, my hands, and my heart.

For those who are unwilling to forgive me, I say, Don't you want to be set free? Don't you want to see what God's mercy sees? Don't you want to give what God gave to you?

Forgiveness. Forgiveness.

During this time, I was actively pouring myself into Bible study at church. It was following a sermon series that truly changed my life. One message from the sermons that was like a resounding gong in my head was, "You are loved more than you could possibly know, and everything is going to be okay. Our gracious Father will not add conditions to His love for us." That is incredibly true. God asks us to follow His book and His ways, and to love Him and one another.

Words like this and talking with my table group on Wednesday nights made me realize we are all broken people. We all have issues, struggles, and skeletons in the closet; even if we don't want to face them, they are there! One of the ways forgiveness entered my life was to realize I had to forgive myself for my sins and my sin patterns, past and present, and to live in the way Christ tells us to live in the Bible. We can always excuse our sins; there is always a way to excuse our sin. But to live in Christ, we have to admit those sins to Him and then start to let them go. As hard as it may be, we have to relinquish our sins. We cannot say we are living with Christ and continue to sin. We just can't. And as hard as life was about to become, I needed to let go of all my sin patterns. Even if it meant people would be hurt.

## *February 6, 2015—Greater Is the One*

What does "Greater is the one living inside of me, than he who is living in the world" mean to you? I'll tell you what it means to me. My first memory of not being good enough was in the fifth grade. I was a new student to the school I was attending, and believe me, I was not pretty. The kids on my bus were not kind. I was chubby to say the least, with buck teeth, and the kids on my bus totally loved (note the sarcasm) that about me. It was nothing to hear for the entire thirty-minute bus ride, "Hey, Bucky, what are you doin' on the bus? Shouldn't you be in your habitat? Hey, Bucky, why don't you crawl back under the ugly rock. Hey, you fat, buck-toothed, stupid girl, go back to the zoo." I would feel wads of spit or paper spitballs in my hair. When this was brought to the attention of the people who were supposedly entrusted to care for me, I was told, "I don't want to stir up any trouble in the neighborhood. Just learn to deal." This went on for the entire seven years I rode the school bus, every day to and from school, which made me very tired.

I also learned through the years that for some, I would never be enough. The "Why can't you be more like …?" soon grew weary, and I always searched for that one person here on earth who would be like God. By that, I mean a person who would love me unconditionally and forever. I learned, after telling a friend about child abuse I'd survived from the ages of three to sixteen, that sometimes these things need to be kept quiet because they were shameful. At a very early age, like I've already stated, I learned to think for myself, read by myself, listen to God's voice by myself, and sometimes even have little conversations inside my head with God, telling Him, "Hey, I am okay, right?" I would hear God say back, "Yes, you are just fine. You are Mine; you are wonderfully made."

But sometimes God's voice is overpowered, and you start to believe the bad over the good. Because if your own earthly family doesn't see the wonderful things you have inside you, who will? This lack of self-confidence and feeling I wasn't good enough, that any idea I'd ever had, any thought I'd ever voiced, every dream I'd had, when voiced, was shot down, brought a certain amount of self-doubt: "You truly are not good enough." I never knew how all this truly affected me until I was about thirty-five, being more and more involved in church. Then it hit me: yes, I am good enough, my dreams are great, I have ideas, and I have feelings that matter. I talked to God, read some scripture, made a change, and started living again. I was really living, really loving, and being loved back … until forty-eight days ago. Then I was feeling lower and lower until one day the song "Greater" by Mercy Me came on the radio. I had heard it many times and would sing it at the top of my lungs, but the words wouldn't entirely hit me until my daughter left my home unexpectedly. For forty days, I beat myself up and listened again to the voices in my head telling me I wasn't good enough. I even listened to my daughter say out loud, "This is going to hurt, but we put on a pretty good show for the past four years." Seriously, you're telling me, and want me to believe (like others before you) that I am not good enough to be your mom? You don't love me or care about me? Wow. Those are harsh words spoken from a child. How do you respond to that? You respond like God would. "It's okay, my child, if you feel that way. I was not putting on a show. I meant every kind word, every gesture, every act of love I did for you, like working three jobs to make ends meet, doing all the household chores so you could concentrate on school and friends, bringing every meal to you when you were at an extracurricular activity, giving every gift I bought with thought behind it, providing every donut and ice cream run, and every morning I took you to school and sang songs together, especially our favorite, "Super Trooper" by ABBA. I treasured every late night I spent waiting for that text to come get you. I meant it all. I would do it all again, if it made your life easier. I would move the entire universe to show you my love, and why? Because God showed me how to love. Did I say there would never be days when we would be at odds? No. Did I say I would never get on your nerves? No. Did I say we would always like each other? No. Did I ever say, "I would only love you if ...?" No. Did I ever say I was perfect and wouldn't make mistakes? No. But like God loves me unconditionally, I love you. I love you when you are near to me, and when you are far away. I love you when you love yourself, and when you don't. I love you when you call out my name for help, and when you want to handle life on your own. I love you even when you hate me. And isn't that what God does? God didn't tell us following Him would be easy and that every day would be full of sunshine and happiness. God did tell us, however, "The holy spirit produces this kind of fruit in our lives: love, joy, peace, patience, kindness, goodness, faithfulness, gentleness and self-control. There is no law against these things" (Galatians 5:22–23 NIV).

Wow. I guess that's why the song "Greater" means so much to me. There always has been, and always will be, someone who doesn't like me, who doesn't love me, who says I am not good enough. Truly, all people want their family to love them unconditionally, without boundaries, without stipulations, without the feelings of "I'll love you if ..." But, sometimes that is not a reality. I guess that's why God and I are together so much. God tells me, "Bring your tired [I have many times], bring your shame [I have, over my own abuse as a child, over my failed marriages, over the lack of honor and respect I feel from my earthly family], bring your guilt [I have over every mistake I have made, ever sin I have committed], and bring your pain [I have over every time I have reached out to be rejected] Don't you know? That's not your name, and you will always be much more to Me."

Every day, I do wrestle with the voices that keep telling me I'm not right, but it is all right. I've brought my doubts (over every decision I have ever made that directly affected the life of another), brought my fears (over every step I took when God asked me to take to better my life), and brought my hurt (oh, my God, how many times have I bought my hurt to Him?). There'll be no condemnation here. God says I am holy, righteous, and redeemed. (Seriously? No condemnation? No pointing out my mistakes, my wrongdoings, my trespasses?) Every time I fall (which is often), there'll be those who call me a mistake. (Shall I start naming names in just the past week?) No, it's okay. Why? "Because I hear a voice, and He calls me redeemed, when others say I'll never be enough, and greater is the ONE living inside of me" Yes, I truly hear the voice of God. I spend every morning, every lunch, every dinner, and every bedtime with Him. I told my table group just last night that I don't have that one aha moment, when God slapped me in the face and I turned away from a life I should not have been living. I grew up in a wonderful church and started teaching Sunday school in another. I have surrounded myself with good Christian people, and even some sinners who have not yet started to believe. By my earthly family, I have been made to feel worthless, been persecuted for loving everyone, and been so full of pain and anguish, I literally cried out to God, "Why, why, why am I not loved on earth as I am in heaven?" I've even questioned His decision to "knit me in my mother's womb," questioned why He would bring me into this world to live a life full of questions, condemnation, and persecution. Why would He do this? I decided maybe, just maybe, that was my cross to bear. Maybe my walk with God and feeling persecuted, rejected, and condemned by my earthly family was meant to bring me even closer to God, to keep the fruit of the Holy Spirit alive inside and to show anyone else walking the same walk I have walked that we are never alone. We have a greater name, we have a greater love, because as 1 Peter 2:4 states, "As you came to Him, the living Stone—rejected by men, chosen by God, are precious to Him. I am precious, I am loved, and I thank Mercy Me for recording this song because it touched my heart in a way I can't really explain. Sometimes you must experience the message a song or a book gives your heart. I can run freely because I truly see how God sees me, and that makes me love Him more and more. My

God is greater than he who is living in the world. Yes, He is greater, He is greater than he who is living in the world.

I also learned during my Wednesday night table group Bible study that grace was waiting for me to reach up and grab it! My Father was waiting for me to fall into His arms and feel the peace that He had to offer. I could rest in the truth that Jesus heard my prayers, and He knows humans are fickle and flawed. He is for me and really wanted to help. I simply needed to cling to His hand and not let go. This was a difficult concept for me to grasp. I wanted to reach out and grasp His hand and never let go, but I was also so afraid of rejection. Would God reject me as others had, or would God fully accept me, flaws and all? If I admitted my sins but did not stop the pattern of sin, would God still accept me into His family, or did I have to be perfect from the get-go? If I asked Him every day to forgive my sins, before and after the sin, would He still accept me? If I continued to ask for His help in ridding myself of my sin pattern, would He still love me? Would He still help me? The answer is a very loud yes!

## *February 16, 2015—Psalms and Sadness*

Lord, how long will You forget me? Forever? How long
will You hide your face from me? (Psalm 13:1 NIV)

It has now been almost two months since I have seen my daughter. I feel sad. While I've been walking this journey, I have sought the counsel of many: God, my family, my friends who welcomed me with open arms, my counselor, my minister, a youth minister, my senior minister, the director of my Sunday school group, my boss, my co-workers, my neighbor, my "work daughter," and God again. All these folks have advice, and it conflicts with my heart and my head on a continual basis. Their advise comes in many forms and I'm sure you're hearing it too:

"Stay strong. It's not you; it's her. Don't let her see you sad, don't let her weigh you down, don't let her consume your thoughts. Stay in contact with her. Send her cards, write her notes, send her e-mails. Don't talk to her. Quit e-mailing, stay silent. Do what your heart tells you to do. Open your door and heart to her, keep reaching out. Focus on who does love you. Search your heart and what you may have done wrong. Pray. We'll pray for you, and we'll pray for her. Pray for wisdom and guidance. Pray for God to show you what you've done wrong. Don't be sad (the Lord is my shepherd; I shall not want). Don't worry (I will fear no evil). It may be years before you see her again. She will contact you soon. She will need you. Something will happen that will remind her of you." Should I go on? Does any of this help?

Well, I've prayed for wisdom, and I'm still as dumb as I was yesterday. I have prayed for guidance, and yes, I still need my guide dog. (He guides me in the paths of righteousness, for His namesake.)

I've prayed for God to show me what I've done wrong, and I've even confessed all my sins for the past twelve years to about as many people. (He leads me besides still waters, He restores my soul.)

So far, nothing has worked.

So, I am sad.

I am sad because I've been smacked in the face with the reality I already knew: sometimes those who say they are Christian do not act in a way Jesus would want them to act, and to me, this is sad. (He prepares a table in the presence of my enemies; He anoints my head with oil.)

I am sad because I am being persecuted for normal mother-daughter issues that should not be blown into the mess they are now. You see, I was always told, "You are a single mom. I've raised two daughters, and I know how kids are, so if you need help, just ask." I did just that, and I am being punished for it. And after thirty days of not speaking to two, and fifty days to another, these people see nothing wrong with what they did or what they have done. They don't even have a clue what the truth is.

I am sad because I put my heart, soul, and life into a child. My world revolved around what she wanted out of life and what I could do to help her life be easier, and I am being punished for it.

I am sad because everywhere I go, I look for her, and she is nowhere to be found. I want so badly to put my arms around her, hear her voice, laugh with her, cry with her, rejoice with her, listen to her stories, go shopping with her, listen to what she wants for her future, and do all the things we used to do. They are gone.

I am sad because I was the single mother of one, and now I have none. (Even though I walk in the valley of the shadow of death, I will fear no evil, because you are with me.)

I am sad because I have searched my heart. I have mailed her cards, clothes, Christmas gifts, money, and a valentine with a coffee gift card—all with no response or even an ounce of forgiveness.

I am sad because after talking with fellow parents of "lost children," it may be years before I ever see my daughter again.

I am sad because I miss her.

I am sad because I love her.

I am sad because the reality is she does not miss or love me.

I am sad because knowing all this and feeling all this is overwhelmingly sad. (Surely goodness and love will follow me all the days of my life.)

I will dwell in the house of the Lord forever, because there is great peace, comfort, and love with Him.

## *February 17, 2015—Loving and Moving Forward*

Move on, move forward, keep your chin up, keep doing what you're doing. It's all you can do, and it's what everyone says to do. Move forward. Move on. Don't let her see you sad because she is gone; that's what she wants. Okay, I cannot let her know I'm sad, worried, upset, angry, confused, and feeling quite rejected … The question I have is, How?

When I saw Aurora, she seemed mad and asked how could I not want to work on our relationship. My question to her would be, "I have been trying to work on it. You, however, are not giving me the time of day. I have called, written, sent cards, tried to find you on social media, called one of your friends to find you, filed a missing and endangered adult report, and contacted every so-called adult I know to find out what's going on with you. And what have you done in return? Turned off your phone; blocked me from finding you on Facebook, Twitter, and Instagram; and refuse to answer any of my requests to get counseling together. Yet you accuse me of not wanting our relationship. Then you do the ultimate: you tell me you do not love me or care about me and our life has been a lie. Wow. So faced with all your 'truth' and rejection, I should be able to move forward, right?" I mean, she definitely let me know that as a mom, I have failed her by working so she wouldn't have to, buying her a car, taking her to the beach, cooking all her meals, doing her laundry, and taking care of everything inside and outside the house so she didn't have to … Oh, every now and again, she would change out the laundry or scrub my bathroom, or run the vacuum, wash a few dishes, or load or empty the dishwasher. So certainly I should be able to be relieved (as she said she was because she had left the nest, so to speak), I should be able to move forward, right? Move on, right? Forget I was ever a mom, right? Wrong. Because I am not made like her, I cannot stop being a mom like she can stop being a daughter.

One of my coworkers tells me this is my new normal. I guess she is right. However, this new normal doesn't feel so normal. It feels about as un-normal as possible. How do you stop being a mom? How do you forget about your child? How do you move forward when your child is in the same town as you, but you cannot find her or contact her? I can't even get so-called adults to give me her phone number. I don't even want to call her or text her; I simply want some sort of connection to her. I'm trying to carry on, so to speak.

I am so used to rejection that I should change my last name to just that: Lucy Rejection. I have had enough conversations with ministers, coworkers, and friends that I sound like a broken record. So in the hope of healing, I have decided to change her bedroom: a fresh coat of paint should do it some good, some new furniture, and remove all the special knickknacks I have given her and the special wall art I picked out especially for her. I even had a small change of pace for me and took a mini vacation. Did any of that work? Nope. And why not? It's because of my love for her. When you truly love someone, you cannot forget her, or move forward without her, or feel she no longer exists. I read several Bible passages, and I think this one says a lot:

> If I speak in tongues of men and of angels, but have no love, I am only a resounding gong or a clanging symbol; if I have the gift of prophecy, and can fathom all mysteries and all knowledge, and if I have faith that can move mountains, but have not love, I am nothing. If I give all I possess to the poor and surrender my bodies to the flames, but have not love, I gain nothing. Love is patient, love is kind, it does not envy, it does

not boast, it is not proud, rude, self-seeking, not easily angered, it keeps no records of wrongs. Love does not delight in evil but rejoices with the truth. Love always protects, always trusts, always hopes, always preservers. Love never fails … and now these three remain: faith, hope and love. But the greatest of these is love. (1 Corinthians 13:1-8, 13 NIV)

I cannot stop being a mom, I cannot stop the love I have for my child, and I cannot put conditions on my love for her. I don't understand people who can put conditions on their children. Now, in certain circumstances, when a child may be a drug addict, alcoholic, or child abuser, I understand conditions. But when you love something with all your heart and soul and have made sacrifices for that child, how does that make you a bad person? After talking to several ministers, I see I am a good person and a great mom, and I have so much unconditional love in my heart. And not just for my child—I love my friends, coworkers, neighbors, and adopted family like they truly are my own. How does anyone not love this way? And believe me, I know I am not perfect (I have parents, a sister, and two ex-husbands to tell me how imperfect I am), and God knows I have sinned. God also knows I have been judged by choices I have made, by my mistakes and my life, from the very first breath I took when I entered this earth.

I am blessed and thankful, however, that God in heaven knows my heart and sees who I am. As 1 Corinthians 16:13–14 (NIV) says, "Be on your guard, stand firm in the faith, be men of courage, be strong. Do everything in love."

Therefore, I will be on guard for my enemies and the devil speaking in my head, telling me I will not survive without Aurora. I will stand firm in my faith and hold strong to the hope that someday she will regret this time apart and be a woman of courage to come ask to reconcile our relationship. I will be strong and persevere and know it's okay to laugh, smile, be angry or sad, and have the doubts in my mind. And most of all, I will do everything in love … for if not for God's love and His command to love one another, where would we be?

Praying simple prayers became a huge part of my life. I prayed in the shower, in the car, in the bathroom, in the lunchroom at work, and while standing at the copier at work. I would pray for God to change my heart, to change Aurora's heart, and to change my family's heart. I would pray every time I woke up at night, and I often prayed myself back into a deep slumber. I'm sure being in God's presence brought that bit of peace. It was the beginning of my heart change toward everyone. "Lord, change my heart." So simple, so powerful. But these small, simple prayers eventually led me to believe and cling to hope that someday, my family would be together again. I would have the family God wanted me to have, I would have the love God wanted me to have, and I would see myself as He saw me, broken yet beautiful.

## *February 20, 2015—Keeping the Joy during the Sad Times … or as I Like to Call Them, Blessings*

"We pray for blessings, we pray for peace." Yes, you can hold on to your joy during the sad times. I know you can, because I do have the joy of Jesus in my heart. Funny, huh? What's funny about this is a statement my boss made to me today: "And if you did that, you would be happier." I understand what he was saying. I sound like a bitter old woman at times, especially when I talk. And maybe when I am writing about this pain I am feeling, I probably seem like Charlie Brown: "I'm doomed." But I know I'm not because I do have faith. And I do have many blessings, so today I will talk about them.

"Comfort for family, protection while we sleep." One big blessing is my boss, and the law office I work with, which is full of amazing people. I'm sure you are thinking, "You are calling lawyers amazing?" Yes, my dear reader, they are amazing. My boss has taken me from a beat-up, self-confident-lacking, "I'm just a piece of the puzzle" type of worker to someone who finally sees her self-worth in the workplace, and now I know I do play an important part in the cog of a wheel. He is a Christian whom I admire for his honesty and integrity. He's a wise man. I can discuss with him any problem in the world, and he will give me not only his life experience but also his honest opinion on anything … and I do mean anything. Without his support, I know I wouldn't be where I am today. To sum up my feelings toward him, I refer you to 1 Thessalonians 5:12–14. "Now we ask you brothers to respect those who work hard among you, who are over you in the Lord and who admonish you. Hold them in the highest regard in love because of their work. Live in peace with each other. And we urge you brothers, warn those who are idle, encourage the timid, help the weak, be patient with everyone."

When you think of him, you also think of his wife. Not only is she a fellow coworker, but she is also a friend. I don't know her entire life story, nor do I need to, but she is that person who makes you feel welcome the first moment you meet her. Her crazy antics, her contagious laugh, and her gift of giving for no reason will undoubtedly make you realize you can call on her for anything— painting, drinking a glass of wine, shopping (our favorite pastime, but don't tell her husband when we go!), sharing a great meal, floating in a pool and talking about life, or putting together furniture. She is a great woman whom I am honored to call my friend, and she is my sister through Christ. She has been a wonderful support through all my struggles and joys. We have raised daughters together, and although our girls are all unique individuals, the struggles are still the same, the joys tripled. She has paved the path for me to walk behind her regarding how to be a great mom. She gives her honest opinion if you ask, and her advice is truly treasured. She has hugged me when I've cried and continuously tells me I am strong, even when I feel so weak, and especially during my most recent loss. Proverbs 17:17 is her: "a friend loves at all times."

Then there is the first person I ever met as an adult. We taught Sunday school together, we exercised together, and she named me the "Walking Nazi" because when we would walk together, I would get mad or excited about something I was talking about and walk faster and faster. She has included me in just about every aspect of her kids' life, and she has included me in family functions, holiday meals, and family pool parties. She was there for me every moment of my daughter's life—the good, bad, her cancer days, her struggles with my divorces, and all those moments of teenage angst. Her family welcomed me with open arms, and I love each of them like I truly am their long-lost aunt. I know, without a doubt, she will correct me when I'm wrong and call me out when I have walked a not-so-correct line. She truly is my Romans 9:25. "I will call them my people, who are not my people, and I will call her my loved one, who is not my loved one." If I could handpick a sister, she would be it! She never ceases to amaze me with her strength.

And then there is the Paul to my Saul, or the Saul to my Paul. She calls me out on my sinful nature, she does not judge me, she speaks truth to me in love all the time, and she sees my very soul sometimes. Although this can be scary, she believes in me, supports me, and listens with her heart. I don't even have words to explain what she means to me. She is definitely my John 3:21. "But whoever lives in the truth comes into the light, so that it may be seen plainly what he has done has been done through God." She keeps me grounded and focused on God.

There are neighbors, other friends, and distant family members for whom I am so grateful. The family who lives next door with two boys whom I have adopted as my nephews. My neighbor I call Mom, who helps me with outdoor projects and gives the best hugs, and even though we have only known each other for seven years, I feel I've known her all my life because our lives intersect and seem so alike, I can only believe we are soul sisters. There is my one friend I have followed from New Albany to Sellersburg who always brings sunshine to any day, and her smile and her stories make me feel at home. She has also seen me at my worst of times and best of times, and she always lifts me up, even during her saddest moments. She makes me feel better, she is unique and beautiful, and she is my friend, Carol.

Last, but not least, there is my Naomi. There is always that one person you open up to finally, after years of holding in all the bad. "What if my greatest disappointments, or the aching of this life, is the revealing of a greater thirst this world can't satisfy?" There is the one person who sees you at the best of times and worst of times, who saves you times and time again—not just figuratively but literally. She saved me from an abusive marriage, made me see I was worth more than what I was receiving, and kept me from self-destructing, from going crazy, from checking out when I wanted to check out. She has held me up when I have cried too many times to count. She has forced me to get up every day during some pretty trying times and told me to pull my act together, go to work, and stay the course. "What if your healing comes through tears?" She tells me—like everyone above—that I am worthy no matter what anyone in my past has ever said. She has stayed up late with me to talk, even when I repeated myself a hundred times, and she has supported every dream I've ever had. She also includes me in any family gathering, and her family has accepted me and loved me like I never knew family could love. She loves my friends and has the biggest heart I've ever known. She nurtures, cares, loves everyone, and supports her family and friends equally, with no judgment and no expectations. She is my Ruth 1:16. "Don't urge me to leave you ... where you stay, I will stay ... your people will be my people."

So you see, I have many blessings, and I recognize them, appreciate them, and love them unconditionally. I don't judge them, even during terrible pain, when I know I seem I lack joy and seem angry, bitter, and unhappy—"the rain, the storms, the hardest nights." When you are surrounded in every aspect of your life by people who love unconditionally, who show you and tell you, "You are worth my time!" When you are at your lowest and think you are all alone, these blessings overflow your heart with love and life.

Eventually, we learn that freedom starts with becoming aware of our own cover-ups. We must learn to accept our habits, our blind spots, and the hidden places in our hearts. Whatever our issues may be, someone else is probably experiencing, has experienced, or is about to experience what we just walked through. It's our duty to cling to one another and, as my church states, walk therewith. What a joy to have comfort of someone who is as imperfect as me! I felt alone, but now I know my situation was not as unique as what my earthly family wanted me to believe.

I was happy to read that God's love would always find a way into our darkness. I needed to know God met me wherever I was—happy, sad, joyful, angry. I felt so alone in my own skin, but I kept telling myself God was with me. While lying in Aurora's room in the dark, I would have imaginary conversations with God and imagine Him sitting on the edge of the bed, holding my hand, and talking.

March 5, 2015, was my then best friend's birthday, and I was willing myself to want to celebrate. It had been seventy-three days since I had seen my daughter, and I was slowly losing steam, or so I felt. How could I continue to go on? How could I continue to live without her? I had spent every day living for her, so now what?

## March 5, 2015—Words Can Break Us Down; Words Can Build Us Up!

"They've made me feel like a prisoner, they've made me feel set free, they've made me feel like a criminal, made me feel like a king." —Hawk Nelson, "Words"

Words can make you a prisoner of yourself. There is also the guilt we hold for things said in the wake of a journey, either to find ourselves or maybe to help others find their path. Someone else's words can be perceived to make us feel bad and as if we have done something wrong, yet other words can raise our spirit so we feel like royalty. Have you ever noticed when you talk to some people, they are so positive and uplifting that you feel on cloud nine when you leave them? Others can take you back to dark places in your life when they speak. I know several of those, and when speaking to them, they draw me into their cave of despair or make me feel as if I am a toddler.

How many hours have you spent analyzing a conversation and wondering if the people you were speaking with were trying to build you up or break you down? I have come to realize I mainly have had relationships with people who constantly make me question my ability to function as an adult, try to manipulate me, turn a situation to be only my fault, make me question my intelligence, and definitely reject the truth I am trying to speak. Ephesians 4:15 says, "Instead, by speaking the truth in love, we will grow to become in every aspect the mature body of Him who is the head, that is Christ."

It took me a long time to fully comprehend what this verse really means. You see, I always thought it meant if someone explained to me the error of my ways and how you're my point of view, thinking, or perception was wrong, they were automatically correct. After studying this verse, however, I now realize the point of this verse is to bring us all to the unity of faith, bring us all together as one, and have a good conscience. Those people should be ashamed when they falsely accuse you. Your reply to someone speaking the truth to you in love should be gentle and respectful. After speaking to my minister and therapist about all this, I now understand that sometimes people can speak to you like you are a criminal or toddler because of their own immaturity. I also now understand that to be mature is not just an age or experience. To be mature, you experience spiritual and emotional growth. Without it, when someone speaks words of truth to you, they normally will tear you down or put out the fire in your heart. This is done because some people in our lives do not want to see us grow and become closer to other people or to our God. How sad for these people. After speaking very candidly to my minister, I know I am not only emotionally healthy but spiritually healthy as well because I can see the two sides of every coin. I have always wanted relationships to be reconciled. Nonetheless, sometimes, these two aspects of health never develop in some people.

I do not have too many people in my life who wish to see me emotionally healthy, or even realize I am, and they project their own baggage and issues on me. Okay, so is that my problem or theirs? It's theirs.

What I've also learned, time and time and time again, is only God can heal the heartache, only God speaks over the fear, and only God's voice is what I need to hear. It's taken quite a hike over the past eleven—yes, eleven—years to fully come to this realization. I've listened too often to others, taken to heart and beaten myself up over what they have said, come pretty darn close to taking my own life, and searched and searched my heart to hear what is really true. When I talk to my minister and my counselor, however, it's becoming a shorter and shorter time for me to come to terms that I am not the only person with problems, and sometimes the problems aren't even mine to carry. It's on others. How freeing is that? Yes, I said it once, and now I am going to say it again: I am not the only person with problems or issues! And the more I regain my own strength and realize I am in Him and He is in me, and that His grace is the loudest sound I hear, the stronger and brighter is the fire in my heart.

I've learned unresolved pain keeps us dead inside. We learn to protect ourselves and become detached. I learned to become aware of what God wanted to show me by embracing the only person who could liberate me from the pain: Jesus. He invited me to rest, reflect, repent, and try to reconcile my life before I could reconcile with anyone else. He gave me quiet moments and mercy. I could, as it was easier, continue to cling to the earthly beings that professed their love for me, but when I did this, I continued to feel empty inside. I could hear their words, but there was a deep longing inside me for something more, for someone to heal all the hurts and wounds of my past. But no earthly being can heal us. We must look to heaven to the one who is the author and perfecter of all: God.

## *March 21, 2015—Guarded. Grounded, and Gearing Up!*

"Human beings are poor self-examiners, subject to superstition, bias, prejudice, and a profound tendency to see what they want to see rather than what is really there." —M. Scott Peck

I recently joined this group at church called table groups. It's a more in-depth study of our Sunday sermon, and study was followed up by a group called Equip. Equip was a study that dove into the Bible and helped us learn whether we were followers of Christ or just fans, and I am definitely a follower with a hunger to learn more and dive in deeper to bring myself closer to Him. Why? What has He done for me? I mean, really, I'm a survivor of child sexual abuse, a survivor of rape, and a survivor of an emotionally and physically abusive marriage. I've never had high self-esteem, I've struggled with my weight, and I suffered from bulimia for about twenty years. Now, I am finding myself alone again, an empty nest without my child, without parents, and without my sibling—not by my choice but by theirs. But what has stayed constant during all this has been God's everlasting, perfect, constant, never-ending love.

I recently had a conversation with someone and was telling him how, until I knew him, I had never experienced the feeling of having someone say the words to me, "I'm sorry." Period.

Not "I'm sorry, but if you hadn't ..."

Not, "I'm sorry, but you shouldn't have ... and then I wouldn't have ..."

Not "I'm sorry, but you started it ..."

Just "I'm sorry." Those were foreign words to me, and it took me a very long time before I could realize they were meant. It was an even longer time before I could hear them and not be waiting for the explanation of why *sorry* came with no *but* after it.

I shouldn't be surprised however, by my past experiences with *sorry*. Kyle Idleman writes of this "blame game" mentality in his book *AHA*. It goes back as far as Adam and Eve. In Genesis 3:12, Adam blames Eve for his sin of eating from the tree of knowledge. He doesn't take personal responsibility for his actions. So why should I be surprised no one in my life can do so? I was also explaining to someone recently why I've always been an observer in life. I've never quite been good enough, pretty enough, strong enough, sporty enough, tall enough, or short enough. There was always something lacking, something never quite enough. I was not good enough, which fed into my insecurities, so I remained the quiet observer.

Now, I fully understand God truly did make me this way, and He certainly loves me just the way I am. And so do I. I've also learned through the Table Group and the Equip sermon series that we are all human, and we do make mistakes. We try to live in the word, and stay in the word, remain in the word, and remain in Him. We do live in the world, but we do not have to *become* the world. John 15 is such a beautiful chapter about being in God and Him in us. It mentions remaining together eleven times. Can you believe that's all we have to do? Just stay in the word. Stay with Him. He stays with us. How hard is that? He is the vine, and we are the branches; we bear His fruit, and we continue to grow. His command to us? Love one another. How hard is that? The more I think about this, the more I start observing again. The more I start observing, the more I want to start gathering those I love around me and sharing their stories. Then I start reaching out to others who are hurting, spreading the hope to those who feel hopeless. I've been hopeless. I've let down God by feeling hopeless, and for that I apologize to Him. I did not mean to doubt His great power. So I asked for forgiveness and gently reminded myself of Philippians 4:6. "Do not be anxious about anything, but in everything by prayer and petition, with thanksgiving, present your requests to God." And He gently reminds me in Philippians 4:7, "The peace of God which guard your heart and mind in Christ Jesus." I know He forgives me my doubts, I know He knows my heart, and I know He has my request taken care of before I even ask it.

Because of my life experiences so far, and because of this great revelation, I've decided to renew my vow to Christ. I've decided to rededicate myself to Him and be rebaptized. Now, I know it isn't necessary to be dunked again, but I really want to do this symbolic gesture for myself and for God. I want to wash away the past twenty-seven years of my life and renew my spirit, my hope, and my faith. I want to feel the rebirth of His love. My life has changed so much in the past few years. And for the first time in a very long time, I finally feel my life has purpose and meaning. I told my therapist as much today, as well as telling her for the first time in my life, "I know God made me, God loves me, and Jesus wants to be my best friend. God knows I am worth giving His only Son to die for me. No matter what any other person on earth thinks of me, God loves me and knows my value. I thank Him for this, and all I want to do now is serve Him and show Him how thankful I am for His perfect love." I remain guarded of my new heart and grounded in this verse from 1 Thessalonians 5:16–18, "Be joyful always; pray continuously; give thanks in all circumstances, for this is God's will for you in Christ Jesus." I remain in Him.

From my Bible study notebook:

What have I learned about myself? I am loved and worth living. For so long, I felt I wasn't worth anyone's time, anyone's consideration. Now I was beginning to see at times I was worth time and attention. I discovered I had great friends around me who cared, who truly loved me for me. It's a slow process, but it is happening.

What have I learned about God? He loves me just as I am with no conditions. He asks only that I am honest and open with Him and rely on Him in every situation. Bad situations are not sent by God, but how I respond to the bad situations is important. I can grow and learn and see what He has in store for me, or I can be bitter and let anger grow and fester. I want to grow and let go.

My one-line prayer to God: Please soften my daughter's heart so she can see how good my life is now.

## *March 27, 2015—Because He Lives (Amen)*

"Because He lives, I can face tomorrow, because He lives, all fear is gone, because I know He holds the future, and life is worth the living, just because He lives." —Matt Maher, "Because He Lives"

I took the K-Love 30 Day Challenge about a year ago, and I'm still listening to nothing but Christian music to this day—in my car, at work, and when lying in the tanning bed. (Yes, twice a week I submit to this guilty pleasure, and I have to tell you, it has improved not only my skin tone and color but also my mood during the winter months. Who knew?). When I am on the elliptical machine, if I'm not reading the Bible, I have my iPod on, listening to Mercy Me, Casting Crowns, Steven Curtis Chapman—the list goes on and on. Sometimes the simple words or simple chorus of a short song can have power we never knew existed.

I heard the words to the song I am referencing today, "Because He Lives" by Matt Maher, and it brings tears to my eyes. I think about the upcoming Easter holiday, and what I am feeling is unexplainable. I like Christmas and the joy and hope, the birth of Jesus. But Jesus rose at Easter—at Easter, He lives! You see, I absolutely love spring, I love Easter, and I believe there is a reason God made my birthday in the spring. He knew I would love spring and all the newness of the season. The renewal of grass, gardens, flowers—oh, how I love when flowers first start poking their little heads up from the mulch, when there are buds on trees. The sunrise and sunset in the spring even seem different.

What I dread about spring and what makes me sad is Good Friday and thinking about how God sent his Son to be nailed to that cross for all my shortcomings and sins, yet God loved me so much that He did this for me and for you! He loved me so much, He wants me to live without sin. He wants me to live by His book and His laws, knowing I would mess up. He still did this one act of such unconditional love, compassion, mercy, and grace. God did this for us.

When I watch the movie *The Seventh Sign,* and I see the scene where Demi Moore's character is giving birth and hears the words, "Would you die for him?" and the scene is flashing between biblical times and present day, and she reaches her hand out and touches her tiny baby boy and hears the words again and says, "Yes, I would die for him," as she holds her baby's hand for that one and only pivotal time, I am moved beyond words. How many of us would die for our children? All of us. How many of us would give our children's lives for the lives of everyone on earth? Read that again. How many of us would give our children's lives for the lives of everyone, every single person, on the face of the earth? What love God must encompass. How huge His love must be, to give His Son for us.

Then comes Easter Sunday. I cannot explain why, but every Easter Sunday, I wake up feeling so joyful. I always have. I absolutely adore Easter Sunday. How exciting it must have been for Mary to come to the grave and see the stone rolled away. How exciting to suddenly see the face of Jesus and touch His hands and feet. So as I reflect on my life over the past forty-seven years, I am beginning to realize that like this beautiful song says, I was dead inside and living in my grave. My entire life, I have spent in my own shame by things that happened to me over the years. Things I was too embarrassed about or ashamed of to even admit they happened to me, much less share them with anyone. I believe at times I was even afraid to admit them to God.

But what I've learned is when you are surrounded by people who truly love like Christ loved, who are both emotionally and spiritually mature, it does not matter what path you have walked. Like Christ, they forgive, show you mercy, and roll away all stones.

And even more important, when you surround your life with Christ and His love, when you live for Him, with Him, and in Him, and He is in You, it doesn't matter what you faced in your past, what your present may hold, or what tomorrow may bring because He lives. That is where you should place your focus. He lives in us and for us. We can face anything. We are washed by His blood, with every fear gone. I'm alive because He lives.

From my personal Bible study notebook:

> You and I can feel the fullness of all our history and bravely stand in our truth. If we can't face our fears, then we can't really change. As we go forward discovering the parts of our hearts that hurt, we should do it with a friend. We need that one friend who knows all our ugly and doesn't judge or reject. It is with these relationships that we grow and heal. Jesus is the only fixer and freedom giver.

## *March 29, 2015—Resurrection Eggs and Four-Year-Olds*

One of my favorite things about church is that I am able to serve in Sunday school, and I have my favorite age group, four-year-olds. There is something about this age: being totally potty trained, minds like sponges, and hearts full of unconditional love. Today is Palm Sunday, so I took my resurrection eggs to church. Truth be told, I took them more for me than them. I love these eggs; they tell the story of Palm Sunday to Jesus's death. In case you have never seen these eggs, this is how they tell the story. They come in a regular carton, like all eggs do, and are colored like normal "bunny" eggs would be. But they are more special then bunny eggs because they hold they story of Jesus.

Egg 1, Blue—Holds the Donkey Jesus rode to Jerusalem.

Egg 2, Light Pink—Silver coins, Judas's blood money

Egg 3, Light Purple—Passover cup, the Last Supper

Egg 4, Orange—Praying hands, the Garden of Gethsemane

Egg 5, Green—Leather whip, Jesus's trial, thirty-nine lashes

Egg 6, Light Yellow—Crown of thorns, mocking of Jesus of "King of the Jews"

Egg 7, Yellow—Nails made into a cross, Jesus's crucifixion

Egg 8, Light Green—Dice, gambling for Jesus's robe

Egg 9, Purple—Soldier's spear, soldier pierced Jesus's side

Egg 10, Cream—Linen wrapping, Jesus's grave clothes

Egg 11, Pink—Stone at the tomb, stone rolled away

Egg 12, Light Blue—Empty tomb, Jesus's resurrection

Oh, how I've used these eggs over the years. You can tell the story of Jesus simply, for younger children, or make it complicated for the older ones. Each egg comes with scripture related to it and a small story explaining why the item was so important to His story. I always let the children play with them for a few minutes before opening them and asking about each one. Then I open them one at a time and explain to them what the egg represents and why it is important to us and our lives.

Today, we opened all the eggs, talked about them several times, and went to our big group and talked about Palm Sunday. We heard our lesson about Jesus riding the donkey and the people waving the palm branches and calling out "Hosanna to the King." We even had "Jesus" walk the hall and wave palm branches. After all was said and done, we again started with the resurrection eggs. The other adult leader and I took turns holding up the eggs and asking the kids what was inside and why. It was amazing how many of them knew what the item was, what it was for, and why people used that item. At the very end of our lesson with the eggs, I asked the kids the following questions.

ME: "So what did the people do on Palm Sunday?"

KIDS: "Waved palm branches and yelled, 'Hosanna to the King.'"

ME: "What happened on Good Friday?"

KIDS: "Jesus died?"

ME: "Why did God send His Son to die for us?"

KIDS: "Because he loves us?"

ME: "What did Jesus save us from?"

KIDS: "Our sins."

ME: "Who went to the tomb on Easter?"

KIDS: "Mary."

ME: "Why?"

KIDS: "To check on Jesus."

ME: "What did she find?"

KIDS: "An empty tomb."

ME: "Where was Jesus?"

KIDS: "He arose!"

ME: "So who is coming next Sunday?"

KIDS (with great excitement): "The Easter Bunny!"

---

Folks, I can't make this stuff up! And this is why I love four-year-olds so much. Sweet, innocent, soak it all in, and give truthful, honest, from-the-heart answers. Yes, they know the moral of this story, and that is the important part. They understand Jesus was born, performed miracles, died, and rose again for us. They understand Jesus did this for us because He loves us. I wonder at what age they will forget this important piece of information and begin to live for themselves instead of living for Jesus. My wish for them is that it never happens. My wish is that they always have the joy and excitement of the empty tomb and that they live for Jesus every day from now until the day they die.

Jesus is so wonderful. He loves us and came for us. He took the punishment for all our sins, and never does He punish us or put conditions or stipulations on us. All He gives is His grace and mercy, His pure and unconditional, love. All he wants is to be our best friend. I'm so happy He is mine.

I hope I planted a small seed today. I told the children to be thinking when they open their eyes next Sunday morning, "Christ arose today, up from the grave. He arose with a mighty triumph over his foes!"

Although they may be more excited over the chocolate bunny in the basket for now, I know someday, as they color eggs with their children, they will be thinking about the resurrection eggs they learned about in Sunday school. I hope it sparks a conversation they can have with their children and grandchildren about a precious gift more satisfying than a hollow chocolate bunny, a gift to everyone willing to receive it: the gift of everlasting life.

---

The angel said to the women, "Do not be afraid, for I know that you are looking for Jesus, who was crucified. He is not here; he has risen, just as he said. Come and see the place where he lay. Then go quickly and tell his disciples: 'He has risen from the dead and is going ahead of you into Galilee. There you will see him.' Now I have told you." So, the women hurried away from the tomb, afraid yet filled with joy, and ran to tell his disciples. (Matthew 28:5–8)

---

# April 5, 2015—What Was God Thinking?

> For you are saved by grace through faith and this is
> not from yourselves, it is God's gift – not from works,
> so that no one can boast. (Ephesians 2:8–9 NIV)

Easter is upon us. Our Savior has defeated death for our sins. But this joyous occasion brings questions to my mind, and I sometimes wonder, Is it okay to ask these questions? There were many players in the death of Jesus, and many people played a role in His death, including us. So as Judas betrayed Jesus, what was he thinking? Were those few coins worth it to him? As Peter heard that rooster crow for the third time, what was he thinking? Was he ashamed? Was he scared? Was he shocked as he denied the man he'd walked alongside for so long? As the guards mocked Jesus, what were they thinking? Was there one among them who was ashamed of what they were doing? Was there one ringleader, so to speak, or were they all equally participating willingly in this mockery? As Jesus stood before Pilate and Herod, what were they thinking? Were they happy to see this King? Were they afraid Jesus would take their place of power? As for the people who were shouting, "Crucify Him," what were they thinking? To me, they represent every jury in the world today. Pilate says in Luke 23:14–17 (NIV), "And you brought me this man as one who was inciting the people to rebellion. I have examined him in your presence and found no basis for your charges … neither has Herod … as you can see, he has done nothing to deserve death. Therefore, I will punish him and release him." So He has done nothing wrong, yet the crowd had already judged Him and imposed His death sentence. After Jesus had been beaten, mocked, and made to carry a cross, the guards came across Simon of Cyrene and made him carry Jesus's cross. What was this man thinking? Was he sorry for Jesus? Was he angry with Jesus for having to carry the cross? Was he hoping he would not be crucified too?

And Mary Magdalene. What was she thinking? Here, her friend, probably the only man to show her honest love and compassion, was placed on a cross. I can only imagine the pain in her heart. How sick in her stomach she must have felt. I can't even imagine she could see Jesus—how her eyes had to have been overfilled with tears and sadness. This leads to Mary, Jesus's mother. I cannot begin to imagine her feelings on this day. From the day she knew she had been chosen to carry the Son of God, she had to have been both dreading and rejoicing this day. I know rejoicing is a weird word to choose here, but I know when my daughter was very ill when she was three, I dreaded the day she had her bone marrow aspiration, yet I knew the answer (yes, she had cancer) was a relief. I no longer had to question what was wrong, but I could know the end of a long journey was now upon us. (I am in no way comparing myself to Mary; I am simply trying to illustrate why I chose the word *rejoice*.) I don't know how Mary could follow her son on the walk to the cross, stand, watch the nails pierce His wrists and feet, see the mockery of the crown of thorns upon His head, see the soldiers pierce His side, give Him vinegar to drink, and see the blood on His body. I cannot fathom the pain, the anguish. How could she even stand, walk, or move on this day? I even think about her pain, and as a mother myself, I am overcome with sorrow for Mary. I am devastated to even try to think about her pain. And after Jesus died and was removed from the cross, and she could hold her beloved, perfect Son who'd died for so many, I want to weep for her pain. I want to hold her hands, get on my knees in her presence, and explain to her how incredibly sorry I am for all my sins and for every ounce of pain I caused her. I want to wipe away her tears. Lastly, what was God thinking on the day his Son died? God knew how Jesus's life would begin and end even before He walked the face of the earth. When Jesus was in the garden praying to His Father; when God saw His Son being beaten; when God saw His Son being mocked; when God saw His Son given a crown of thorns; when God saw His Son carrying a cross; when God saw another carrying His Son's cross; when God saw His Son being nailed to the cross; when God heard His Son say, "Father forgive them, for they do not know what they are doing" (Luke 23:34); when God saw the soldiers casting lots for His Son's clothes; when God saw the soldiers give His Son wine vinegar; when God saw the soldiers write "King of the Jews" and place it above Jesus's head; when God heard the criminal mock Jesus; when God heard Jesus cry out, "Father into your hands I commit my spirit" (Luke 23:46 NIV), what was He thinking?

I cannot fathom what He was thinking or how He was feeling. I feel breathless when I think of all God gave and did regarding His only Son. Not just the sins of one person, but the sins of every person on the face of this earth. How excruciating this must have been for God. And then for what I guess is the first time, God held His Son. I know I've been without my own child now for about one hundred days. God was without Jesus for, what, thirty-six years? He held him for three days and then gave Him back to rise again. I guess that's why God is awesome. If I ever see my daughter again, I don't know if I would have the strength to give her up after three days. But God did. He sent His Son back to us to show us His everlasting, amazing grace. I cannot believe God did this for us.

When I think of Easter, one of the last things I think about is Mary Magdalene again. Can you imagine going to the grave of the one you love and finding it empty, only to turn around and see Him? I know this Easter has a whole new meaning to me. My heart has changed in ways over the past two years, I know it's Jesus working in me, and I hope He continues to work in me and through me. Of course, this happens only if I am a willing participant, and you know what? After thinking about all this, I am not turning back. No way. I'm all in. I'm not only following, but I'm running to catch up! I know I will continue to ask questions, and I know I will continue to wonder what God was thinking at times. I know God understands my questions are not because I am questioning what He was doing, but because the parent in me cannot fathom giving my child to die for someone else's to live. Not on purpose, anyway. People die every day, and we agree to donate their organs to save a life. But when I think about what God did, well, to me, God gave His entire being just so we could have a chance to know Him. I think if someone loves me this much, I'll spend my days serving and loving Him back. And I guess that leaves me with one last question: What are you thinking?

---

God is love. Perfect love casts out all fear. (1 John 4:18 NIV)

---

Holidays are the hardest without the ones you love. Every day that passed, I did not know where Aurora was, what she was doing, who she was with, or whether she was okay. Was she ill? Was she eating right? Was she lonely? What kind of car was she driving? Was she still in college? How were her classes doing? Was she still dating that guy? Would I ever spend a holiday with her again? These questions eat me up inside. The not knowing is no closure. When someone dies, you have closure. When someone you love is just out there, the no communication and no information is crazy making. I feel crazy. I've been talked about by others who say that I am crazy. I don't think I'm crazy; my therapist and psychologist say I'm not. I've passed all the tests for multiple personality, bipolar, and other psychological disorders. The number one diagnosis: severe depression.

# April 16, 2015—On My Knees

> "I don't know how, but there's power when I'm on my knees." —Jaci Velasquez, "When I'm On My Knees"

I recently decided it was time to maybe start contacting the people with whom my daughter is living. Maybe it's time. Maybe it isn't. But I know in my heart, if I don't make the first move, no one ever will. Since Aurora called me on Good Friday, I've done even more thinking, more counseling, and more church action, and all I can say is her heart still isn't in a happy place. The beautiful girl I raised is not who she is currently. It pains my heart deeply to know this truth.

Therefore, I am taking the steps and reaching out. And as I am slowly reaching, this song keeps playing in my head. And I keep singing and getting on my knees and listening to it and His voice. Nicole C. Mullen definitely says it best: "There are days when I feel the best of me is ready to begin." So I reach out and call my child, and she doesn't answer, but the owner of the home does.

Then there are days, when I feel I'm letting go and flying with the wind, I am learning through laughter or in pain, how to survive. I've loved through my pain over the past four months almost to the day. I've learned more about who I am and what true love is and is not. It is not hiding truth. It is not being asked a direct question and hiding the truth or hiding behind what you are telling yourself is the truth. I get on my knees and keep praying.

It was recently said to me, "Parenting Aurora is over. If she was in a dorm and away at college, none of us would know what she is doing. At least, that's how I think of this." Really? I think to myself, "Well, I guess you can say that because you have direct daily contact with her. You have her cell phone number and her school schedule. You know when she is not with you, she is either at work, at her boyfriend's, or at her friend's house. You can call her and text her. When she gets home, you can hug her, talk to her, and see her. So I guess in a way, you can kid yourself and believe what you want. But the truth is, she is away from her mother, she is hiding from her mom, and you are an accomplice to that truth." So I ended a conversation today because it was making me very sad, and I went to the ladies' room at work, got on my knees, and said a prayer.

I gave a prayer for my heart to continue to heal, a prayer for my daughter's heart to find its way home, and a prayer for the people who are housing my child to see the piece of the pie they make up in this mess.

And I keep praying for a church friend's mother who has been critically ill for several weeks now, experiencing setback after setback.

I talked to a friend today who is sad. She feels the "evil one" at her back, so I figuratively got on my knees and prayed for her. I told the evil one I am at her back, and he needs to go away in the name of Jesus.

I pray because I felt happy and sad the other day. I was able to spend some time the with two boys next door, and the oldest one ran to me and gave me a big hug like he used to do to Aurora. It so reminded me of her, and I could hear him say, "Hi, Aurora," in his cute little voice. I said a prayer for her to remember him and how much fun we had with them with our summertime s'mores parties.

I think I am not ready to take to many big steps, maybe just baby steps. I need to remain on my knees, and in His arms at all times. I have made it four Fridays now without crying, yet I feel on the verge of tears every waking moment. I've remained in His hands, there is power in His presence, and it is in His presence I need to dwell, never leaving. It's not Him who leaves us, it's we who sometimes leaves His presence.

As I complete my journal entry for tonight, I feel somewhat sad, but I know God feels my sadness, and tomorrow morning I'll wake up ready to take on the world again, because in Him I'm learning to survive. I'll be on my knees in His presence all day. I can be by myself or in a crowd; no one needs to know that I'm talking to Him.

I am so humbled and thankful I have God in my life. I do not know where I would be or who I would be without His wonderful mercy and grace. I do not know where I would be without His open arms and answers to prayers before I've even asked. I know I'll remain on my knees. Psalm 19:14 says, "May these words of my mouth and this meditation of my heart be pleasing in your sight, Lord, my Rock and my Redeemer." That will be my theme song. Blessings.

From my personal Bible study notebook:

---

Your actions, decisions, beliefs, and next steps are your responsibility. Our history is our history. The enemy is more dangerous than those others ever could be. Our past hurts teach us how to hurt ourselves over and over again. It becomes a vicious cycle. We cannot unsee or unfeel what we've lived.

All our life experiences shape us into who we are today. We truly cannot unsee or unfeel what we have lived. But do we let those moments turn us bitter and angry, or do we use those moments to help others in similar situations? I'm learning to share my experiences with others, and I'm learning I'm truly not unique. Several people have walked in shoes similar to mine, and I have to say, it's quite comforting. I'm sorry for other's troubles but glad to know I'm not alone.

But if we own up to our sins, God shows that He is faithful and just by forgiving us of our sins. (1 John 1:9 NIV)

---

## *May 7, 2015—The Prodigal Mother's Day*

But while he was still a long way off, his father saw him and was filled with compassion for him; he ran to his son, threw his arms around him and kissed him. (Luke 15:20 NIV)

Mother's Day is almost upon us, and I cannot celebrate. I told my mom not to be hurt or upset. I love her and appreciate her, but I cannot celebrate a day when half of me is missing.

I am shattered. My heart is in a thousand pieces, and I know my life will never be the same. When Aurora had cancer, I used to think should she die, I could be at peace because I knew she would be with Jesus, and someday I would see her again. The loss of Aurora now leaves me with an entirely different perspective. I am a mom, yet I have no child. Well, I have a child, but she is my estranged daughter for the moment, living life on her own without any contact with me. Not by my choice, mind you. So that leaves me in a quandary—one I do not wish to celebrate.

Two of my best friends have lost their moms, one recently and the other a few years ago. I wonder how they celebrate Mother's Day. Yes, they have children, and their children will celebrate them, but how painful is it to have a mom and know she is in heaven, yet to be unable to spend the day with her? It leaves me to wonder, Will Aurora realize it's Mother's Day, and does she care she has a mom who loves her, misses her, and would love to celebrate in the old way I loved to celebrate, at the zoo? She certainly skipped my birthday without a peep, so I imagine this day will be the same.

I have an acquaintance who has an estranged son. He is off living life with girlfriend and girlfriend's family and his own son, and he only seems to call mom during times of trouble for himself. He basically acts like his mom is the root of all evil and refuses to acknowledge she lives. But let him find himself in a financial quandary, and she is suddenly a hero. One of her friends tells her, "You love the ones who show you love too." Although I most certainly agree with that statement, it still leaves a huge hole in one's heart.

Nothing and no one can take the place of my child. I am not the perfect parent. Never have been. I too was raised by an imperfect mom who was also raised by a imperfect mom, who was also raised by a imperfect mom, and so the story goes all the way back to the days of Eve, Cain, and Able. I wonder if Cain and Able blamed their mom for their problems? I don't blame my mom for my problems. I see where her mistakes played into what mistakes I didn't want to make, and if I did make the same ones she did, well, I ask for forgiveness. I have both been on the receiving end of "My mom is so great," and now I am at the end of "My mom is horrible. Look at how dysfunctional she made me." I can see where one who thinks like a child would think only the mom is to blame, but doesn't it take two to make a relationship?

I remember being an eighteen-year-old girl myself, having my first real boyfriend, and thinking my parents were too controlling or did not understand anything about my life. But I can honestly say I have never had a time in my life when I wished my parents would go away, or when I wanted to never speak to them again. I guess that's what makes my daughter and me so completely different. I always knew we were different—of course we are; our life experiences are completely different. One certainly is not right or more deserving. One certainly is not above taking blame for failure.

I have been thinking how to describe how I feel to people who mean well by saying, "What are you doing for Mother's Day?" Well, I can't explain it. I am a mom, but I do not have any contact with my child, so am I really still a mom? If your child doesn't want you for a mom, does that still make you a mom? What's the word for a parent who has been completely abandoned by a child? If a parent leaves her child, that child is called an orphan. If you don't have contact with your child for so long, the court can take away all your rights. Now, I know at nineteen, almost twenty, she isn't a child. She is a young adult and is trying to figure out life, and she clearly wants me to realize she doesn't need me, doesn't want me, and clearly thinks love is about "being mad, staying mad, doing what I want, and punishing you." Okay. But what does that make the parent you left?

As I come upon this weekend and ponder my place in the world now, I can't come up with words to describe how I feel. I wish I would have made my last Mother's Day more special so I would have that memory to pull me through. I have almost all the mother-daughter pictures ever taken of us on my desk at work. I think if I pray hard enough and put all my faith in what used to be, maybe somehow and some way, it'll come around again. I will be back to the me I used to be.

Tonight at the gym, while reading the book of Jeremiah, the song "Tell Your Heart to Beat Again" by Danny Gokey came on.

That song is totally me. I am shattered. My heart broke the day she left, and it has continued to break with every minute of time apart from her. I don't live in the house of mom anymore; that door was slammed shut, and not by my choice. I do need to say goodbye to the mom side and tell my heart it is okay to beat.

This is a new beginning. I've never been alone, never been on my own. This is an entirely new journey for me, and the biggest compliment about this new journey was given to me the other day when someone I truly admire told me, "Instead of your Job story tearing you away from God, you've drawn closer." What a compliment, and he was right. I've read more religious books, and prayed and prayed, and searched for answers. Not worldly answers, but spiritual answers. And it's true: I have very loving hands carrying me through. I've been driven to my knees, and words didn't help. I stepped into God's light and grace, and ever so slowly, my heart has started to beat again.

Beginning. I am getting back up and trying to leave my dark days behind. Just because I am no longer a mom doesn't mean I am not still a living, breathing being. My story isn't over. My heart can beat again, loudly. And no, I will never be who I once was. I'll never get back to the me I was before the estrangement, but it is okay. When, and if, this estrangement ends, it will be better than it's ever been. I can say goodbye to where I've been and leave those thousand pieces of my heart on the floor. I will tell my heart to beat, beat, beat and step into the light of grace. This is a new journey, one I am not stepping into alone. Every heartbreak, every one of my scars, is totally a picture of who is carrying me. Love does see further. Heaven is working for my good. I simply need to close my eyes, breathe in His love, His Mercy, and His Grace; and let God continue to be the reason my heart beats. And it will … it will … it will … My heart will continue to beat, and to love. It will continue to carry me to a new beginning …

## *May 14, 2015—Held*

"This is what it means to be held, how it feels when the sacred is torn from your life and you survive." — Natalie Grant, "Held"

It's been twenty-one weeks with no child. I am finally at my wits' end and incredibly lonely without her. I miss every inch of five-feet, two-inch frame (if she really is that tall!). The sadness I feel can only be described as mourning. I mourn for her almost hourly. I tried putting her photos back out, and though I love seeing her smiling face, I am left with the reality that they are all I have left. I know in all honesty, with her biological father's family's, they tend to disown one another and never speak again. I witnessed this happen with my father-in-law and his brother, my father-in-law and my ex-husband, and my ex-husband and three of his five siblings. I know in my heart, December 18, 2014, is probably the last day I'll ever hug her, and February 4, 2015, is probably the last time I'll see her and speak to her in person. Not by my choice but by hers. Some of the family members on his side haven't spoken in twenty years.

I wonder what, in the mind of an almost twenty-year-old, makes you never want to speak to your parent. I was her age once, and as much as my parents got on my nerves, as much as I believed my parents were wrong or misguided, or as much as I thought they had twisted or damaged me and my delicate psyche, I cannot imagine my life without them. They helped shaped who I am today, warts and all.

I am sitting and wondering daily, and I know I should not think about it anymore, but I have no idea how to stop thinking about her. I have other things—work, exercise, Bible study, Sunday school with my four-year-olds, neighbors, friends—to fill my time, but nothing takes her place.

So I mourn. I cry. I think. I mourn some more. I cry. I think some more. And I wonder, Who understands this pain? I read something the other day that if you are married, and your spouse dies, you are widow or widower. If you are a child, and your parent dies, you are an orphan. What do you call a parent who has lost a child? Now, mind you, she is not dead; she is most definitely alive, but she chooses to pretend I do not exist. I mourn the loss of what was, what we would be living now, and my future with her. I understand I must be patient, and the entire situation is in God's hands. But for the moment, I want immediate result and for this pain to end.

Then, yesterday I was on the bike at the gym, and the song "Held" by Natalie Grant came on my iPod. God's little message to me. Granted, the song is about a mother who has lost her infant child, but the message fit in telling us that God holds us in His hands when we mourn. The song also describes how God did not tell us our lives would be perfect without pain, but He did promise to be with us through our pain.

Wow! The promise isn't that my suffering will end, that it will be easy, or that I'll forget what I'm going through. The promise is I am held in my suffering, I'm loved, and God is with me every moment. Never does He leave my side. Second Corinthians 1:3-5 tells us, "Praise be to the God and Father of our Lord Jesus Christ, the Father of all comfort, who comforts us in all our troubles, so that we can comfort those in any trouble with the comfort we ourselves receive from God. For just as we share in the sufferings of Christ, so also our comfort abounds through Christ."

I may mourn for Aurora until I take my last breath, but I can be comforted by knowing Christ is with me. I am promised, and I am held.

Pain often puts us on a chase we may never win. Our minds are filled with the slight possibility of finding those hard-to-locate answers to our sufferings. We wake up every morning thinking, "Today, this will all make sense." We keep chasing for answers because we have to understand the why behind the hurt. We often become bitter as we search for the answers we need. However, we need to learn to surrender the bitterness and let it go, mainly because two thousand years ago, a man took all the injustice of the world upon His shoulders and died on a cross. The elusive chase is over.

# June 1, 2015—Battle for Peace

"Bow before the prince of peace let the noise the clamor cease." —Stephen Curtis Chapman, "Be Still and Know"

Today was all about goodbyes. Just when I thought I was done saying goodbye to people ... I subbed in kindergarten at church and totally enjoyed those kids. It's the class I began my Sunday school volunteering in, and it was the weekend they were promoted to first grade—new rooms for them, and my preschool class now moves up to kindergarten. I had eleven kids, and as each one was picked up by parents and I handed out those graduation certificates, I found myself more emotional, proud yet sad at the same time.

There was one child in particular who, one year ago, was quite disruptive and mean, sat by himself, and didn't want to participate in the lessons. At the time, it made me sad to think we were not reaching him. But today, as I entered the classroom, who should I find but him! He invited me to come play *Don't Break the Ice* with him, and after our lesson and worship time, we handed out popsicles. He brought me his, asked me to open it, and then asked if I wanted to share it with him. How he has grown. As he left the class and I handed him his certificate, he gave me a huge hug.

Now, it's not like they are headed to college; they are just moving classrooms, and I'll see them until they are promoted again. But still, the goodbye and good luck, and the promotion is a sad yet proud moment, and it brought back memories of what used to be.

One year ago, Aurora encouraged me to start teaching again, and she seemed to be so proud to introduce me to the crew upstairs. She even seemed to brag a bit on the fact I used to teach the four-year-olds at another church and how much I love kids. She was right: I do, and I always have. It was one year ago I was also planning her high school graduation party. I was incredibly happy to be planning this party, and I was proud of her and the accomplishments she'd made from kindergarten to high school. It was one year ago we brought home her dog, and she would take that cute puppy in her room to sleep every night.

It was one year ago when I thought my life was so great and everything seemed to be in place. I was looking forward to hearing college stories and watching what Aurora did at Kidtown (a ministry at church she was working with). I looked forward to hearing about what her classes in college were all about, whom she met, and what kinds of new and exciting things she would experience. My, how life has changed …

Since Aurora left five months and thirteen days ago, I've struggled for peace. But I also see the blessings I have been given. If not for these kids I get to love on every Sunday, I don't know where I would be. They bring the love I miss from Aurora. Their smiles and laughter are a reminder of what I had, and I hang on to that … but it doesn't take her place. I know she has probably changed a lot since she left, but I still don't see that God has a hold on her heart, because if He did, I believe we would at least be communicating on some level. She has no idea how much I've changed either. Like others who refuse to communicate with me, she has me in a frame of who she *thinks* I am, not who I've become in the past five months. I thought we would be walking this path together, and because of the fact I am walking it alone (with God by my side, of course), I have gotten stronger in faith, stronger in grace, and stronger in my prayer life. It seems (like the song "Battle for Peace" by Luminate) that I am wearing a trench in the floor from being on my knees both figuratively and literally. I've cried out to God so many times, begging Him for her to come home, for her to at least call, for her to send me an e-mail, a text, anything. But I also know I am slowly losing the war. From what I gather from telephone calls and texts, the people she is living with are monitoring her mail and have decided when God tells them to, they will give her anything I mail. So basically, any way I have to reach out is being blocked. For what purpose? I have no idea. God moves you to do something, and it's blocked. So I've lost that battle, and I've slowly lost that war. I have literally fallen, and the fight in me has slowly drizzled out …

There is something else this song says that is very powerful and relative to these kids I teach. God's love is never earned; it is free. Did you get that? God's love is free.

It's just like these four-year-olds, these kids moving forward to kindergarten: their love is also free. And I have to say, "Thank you," to them. No one knows how much I love seeing their faces come in that door on Sunday mornings and smile, or hearing their answers to questions, or hearing them ask questions. They are so innocent, so spongelike, and they soak in every word of every story. And yes, I am getting a whole new group to love and teach and watch grow in Jesus. I wonder if they know how much I am growing by spending that precious time with them? And how much they remind me of Aurora and how my time with them reinforces the blessings I have been given since Aurora left? God does work in mysterious ways of bringing you to and through.

So what to do with the battle of missing Aurora? That's a tough one. I know in my heart I cannot fight this war any longer. Something stronger than me is keeping us apart, and no matter how hard or often or long I pray, until I give the entire war over to God, I won't win. So as hard as it may be, I have to let go. Oh, yes, you can bet I'll still be praying, but to find peace, I offer this battle to God. And by doing so, I feel at times I'm letting God down because for the moment, He must fight this war without me. I cannot carry this alone, or even be on the front line; He's going to have to shoulder this war alone, He and His army ... As for me, I'm going to fall down. I'm going to fall to the ground. I am, for the moment, going to hold on to Him and trade this battle for peace.

---

Blessed are those who make peace. (Matthew 5:9 NIV)

---

# *June 20, 2015—At His Feet*

This weekend, my life takes a huge turn. Maybe not a huge turn, but a step to declaring to the world (well, maybe just those attending church, but I'm sure the news will spread): I'm getting baptized! Yes, I was sprinkled as a child, completely immersed when I was ten, and then sprinkled again at twenty. But this time is completely for me, because I see now who sees me as worthy of love and peace. I have learned over the past six months who values me, and who sees my pain and carries it with them. I have also learned who sees my joy, and who sees my heart.

It hasn't been an easy road. I've been sad, mad, depressed, happy, and a bundle of mixed emotions. I've learned though counseling, meeting with church ministry, and surrounding myself with those who are humbled at the feet of the cross that everything up to this point in my life has given me the strength, the courage, and the hope of what lies ahead. My life isn't very different from anyone else's. I'm sure there are lots of men and women who have survived sexual abuse, an abusive marriage, divorce, a child with cancer, and the stress of being both mom and dad to a child. I've also learned that it truly does take two people to form and sustain a relationship. If only one person is doing the calling and card sending and has offered oneself up at the most vulnerable stage, then that is not a relationship. Most important, I've learned God is not dead, and God never leaves us. We are the ones who wander far from Him, and maybe at times in my life, I have been called a prodigal child. I've strayed maybe not that far, but I can say that I've tried to handle life on my own, which was not a very smart idea.

So God is not dead. God never leaves. Which leads me to, What do I believe? The answer is a resounding yes! Now, I may not always be able to express what I'm feeling, but I know without one single doubt God is with me, God is for me, and God never leaves us. He just doesn't leave.

I've learned that my old self surrounded herself with those people who were emotionally distant. It's a pattern I learned at a very early age, and when I had that aha moment when I finally took a deep look and figured out that I have truly handled every emotionally difficult situation alone it almost knocked me over. Oh, sure, I prayed and sang songs, but something truly started to change in me around May 2014. Now, I am not saying I've always been emotionally connected to anyone through difficult times, and for that I am sorry and ask for forgiveness. I'm also not saying I handled everything perfectly, but those difficult moments are truly what lead me to this aha moment of my life.

I wrote a letter today to one of the men who are going to baptize me, and it was very emotional for me. I was able to tell him what a strong role model he has been. He didn't ever question my motives or judge me for what I was thinking; he simply directed me to look at Bible passages, asked me questions that I felt were leading me to seek higher counsel, and truly made me think about who I was, who I wanted to be, and who I was becoming. He was an encourager, slowly nudging me to where I needed to rest.

As I stay in this state of reverence, I think about the price Jesus paid for me to live, to form this bond with Him. I see what He truly wants for my life and how He placed every person and created every moment to be present for a reason.

I am neither bound by my mistakes, nor will I continue to beat myself up for them. There is no need to do so. Will I let anyone else do so? No. Through God's grace, I am now a new creation. Like the song I've shared below, I am laying my past at the feet of Jesus. It is not through my own strength I have been able to face myself; it was through God's mercy, strength, and steadfast love. I am now very aware of others and see where the true Christian love can be found. I will not allow myself to be bound by chains, because my shackles are broke, and I've been set free. Does this mean I won't have bad days, be sad, make mistakes, fall short of His glory, be angry, or stumble? Nope, but it certainly means I have something greater than anything here on earth in which to fully put my trust.

Only at the feet of Jesus do I need to dwell. Only at the feet of Jesus will I find the peace that passes understanding. My future is in His hands, and like the loving Father I know Him to be, He will never leave or give me situations I cannot handle with Him walking by my side, paving the way before me or carrying me. If we are all made in His image, there is no emotion He hasn't already felt. He has His eye on the sparrow, so I know He is watching me. He has walked my path and holds my future, and I know it's going to be a great life. "At Your Feet" by Casting Crowns is well worth a listen.

---

"Love breaks our fall; Grace carries us home." —Bob Goff, "Freeway"

---

From my personal Bible study notes:

---

Grace. What a unique word *grace* is. I wonder sometimes if extending grace means we are nice for a moment and then throw that person's mistakes in their face. One thing I do get tired of since reconciling with my daughter and her husband is the mistake I made that constantly gets thrown in my face. It makes me sad she says she forgives me, but I am constantly reminded of things I did wrong as a parent or that embarrassed her. I hope she gets through life with her children never making a mistake or hurting them in any way. I certainly hope if she does make a mistake or embarrasses her children, her flaws are extended grace, and her mistakes are never mentioned.

## *July 15, 2015—Worthy, Flawless, Love*

And whoever doesn't take up his cross and follow me
is not worthy of me. (Matthew 10:38 NIV)

What does this really mean to us to you? To me?

A few months ago, I can honestly tell you I did not understand the meaning of what the words, worthy, flawless, and loved meant. A few months ago, I thought I was the only one who should give love and make others feel worthy, and I had so many flaws that I was not worthy of love. I did not understand that I too was lovable, worthy, and flawless in God's eyes.

Funny how life works out. I have learned, and believe me, it hit me like a ton of bricks. I am totally worthy of love no matter my flaws, and when you are surrounded by good, Christian, loving people, that's exactly what you get.

Now, I by no means mean I am perfect now or need only Christians in my life. I certainly have acquaintances I see once a month, people who in the moment will express concern. But when push comes to shove, they are busy with their own lives to really have concern for anyone else. In the past, to me, this came across as people truly note caring, but through the church, the Bible, and therapy, I have learned those previously in my life may love, but they are by no means showing the love Christ calls us to give.

You see, I was thinking and truly believing I was the only person on the face of the earth with problems, flaws, and mistakes. I thought the reason I have two failed marriages, friends who never call, and family who turn their backs during times of trouble was because I was so worthless, I could never be truly loved.

As my people turned their backs and dug me deeper and deeper into a hole of "You make all the mistakes, and we are so perfect," I felt I was drowning in despair. No matter how I reached out, how many times I said I was sorry, how many times I asked for forgiveness, how many times I strove to meet their demands and did exactly what I said I would do, it would never be good enough. I asked for them to come to church and meet with ministers. I told them the past was the past, and it didn't matter to me. I said I was sorry for everything I had ever done wrong, and I confessed all my sins. I asked for forgiveness for being hysterical when I found my daughter missing and for not knowing how to handle this precarious situation. I sent my phone records when they said I had not been calling like I told them I would, and I asked them to come to therapy with me. Do you know what I got in return? Nothing positive. I got more mean messages, more "We are better than you" attitude, and more feelings of "You'll never be worthy of our love." Okay, I understand. So where do I go from here?

I went to church. I went to therapy. I listened carefully to the words of every Christian song I heard. I read my Bible deeper, I went to Bible study, and I shared my life story with the people at my table. You know what I received at church? You guessed it! Love and forgiveness for my mistakes I was told I was worthy of Christ's love because God sent His one and only Son, and whoever would believe in Him would have everlasting life.

What? God sent His only Son to die for me. Because God loves me? How could this be? How, after years of being the only person the face of the earth who makes mistakes, could I be worthy of God's love? The omnipotent being. The sovereign Lord. The one who made the heavens and the earth. God, who knows all, sees all, and judges all.

He loves me? Yes, God loves me. I had to say it again: God loves me. This thought hit me so profoundly in my winter table groups that I realized I needed to commit myself to God and show Him I see His precious gift and will serve Him for the rest of my days. How could I not? He loves me, sees my worth as His child, and made me flawless.

I talked to the church about being baptized again. Yes, I did it at ten and again at twenty, but the urge to do so again was so incredibly strong, I could not say no. While talking to a minister about this process and explaining to him how I was feeling, I said I didn't feel worthy of God's gift because of my past—but I am. I am also worth love of the earthly family God gave me, but evidently they have their own junk to work out, so I'll let them do it. I'll know God has truly entered their hearts and convicted them of reconciliation when my phone rings. And until that time, I will remain in silent prayer for their hearts and the broken relationships.

God doesn't call us to love "if." God doesn't tell us love is about not forgiving. God doesn't tell us love is about being perfect. God doesn't tell us love is about persecuting others. God doesn't tell us love is about judging someone else's mistakes. God doesn't tell us love is about turning your back on those who don't live up to your standards. God doesn't tell us love is about holding a grudge. God doesn't tell us love is about being disrespectful.

The thirteenth chapter of Corinthians tells us exactly what love is.

---

If I speak in the tongues[a] of men or of angels, but do not have love, I am only a resounding gong or a clanging cymbal. If I have the gift of prophecy and can fathom all mysteries and all knowledge, and if I have a faith that can move mountains, but do not have love, I am nothing. If I give all I possess to the poor and give over my body to hardship that I may boast, [b] but do not have love, I gain nothing.

Love is patient, love is kind. It does not envy, it does not boast, it is not proud. It does not dishonor others, it is not self-seeking, it is not easily angered, it keeps no record of wrongs. Love does not delight in evil but rejoices with the truth. It always protects, always trusts, always hopes, always perseveres.

Love never fails. But where there are prophecies, they will cease; where there are tongues, they will be stilled; where there is knowledge, it will pass away. For we know in part and we prophesy in part, but when completeness comes, what is in part disappears. When I was a child, I talked like a child, I thought like a child, I reasoned like a child. When I became a man, I put the ways of childhood behind me. For now we see only a reflection as in a mirror; then we shall see face to face. Now I know in part; then I shall know fully, even as I am fully known.

And now these three remain: faith, hope and love. But the greatest of these is love.

---

Yes, the greatest of these is love. And I am so thankful, grateful, honored, humbled, joyful, excited, and so many other adjectives I don't even know how to express that I found love, true love. I went into the water of baptism my old, shameful, unloved self, and I came out a new creation, one who is worthy, one who is flawless, one who (despite all imperfections) is loved. Yes, I am loved. And I am waiting patiently with hope in faith soon my daughter will return to me, and I can give her all the love I have found. Not that I didn't give her every ounce of my love before, but she'll be amazed at how much more I love her. I will wait to give my love/ I will wait … and wait … and wait until she comes home.

Until then, you'll find me at the gym reading the Bible on my kindle, or after dinner every night studying the sermon for the week, or at work with a new weekly Bible verse on an index card reminding me how much God loves me and how all He wants in return is for me to love Him and others like Christ loved. I can do that. I am totally capable of love—always have been, always will be. But now, I truly understand what it is to accept true, Godly love. Love is the greatest gift I have ever received—Godly, perfect love. When I look in the mirror now, I see God's love, because He waited for me, held His arms out to me, and accepted me in that big family of His. A family full of compassion, respect, joy, and peace, all added together, equals love. Yes, the greatest of these is love.

Love comes in many shapes, sizes, and forms. The love of my dogs makes me so happy. They are always happy to see me, always wagging their tails and enjoying my times. Even if I yell at them for something they have done wrong, they forget it in a heartbeat and show only love. I truly wish humans could be this way.

## *July 29, 2015—In Him*

"I put my hope in you, I lay my life in the palm of your hand, For I'm constantly drawn to you oh Lord, in ways I cannot comprehend. It's no secret we don't belong here, though set apart by the grace of you, we look for the day when we go to a place where the old become brand new." — Mercy Me – In You, Look, 2000

Years ago, I used to put my hope in my family, my friends, my work, and my hobbies. I would be drawn to things or people and wonder why, considering I had them, I was still so sad, lonely, or unsatisfied. Then, I truly met the one thing that satisfies every need: God. In January, I went to a gathering my church has called table groups. It's a small circle of people who answer questions, pray, listen to a synopsis of the sermon from the previous weekend, and discuss the sermon, the devotionals, and our own daily lives and struggles. Since then, I truly feel a complete transformation of my entire being. How could that be? What am I talking about? I'll be more than happy to tell you!

You see, I have always believed I had to think a certain way, believe a certain way, and have friends only from this walk of life, and that most certainly isn't true. I was programmed, whether by my own volition or by listening to others, that I was not worthy of love, my problems didn't warrant compassion, and I would never live up to the standards of those around me. During this discussion session, where I came to talk about some extremely painful issues for me, I discovered something amazing. Jesus used more of the unworthy to spread His good news than saints!

Unworthy people Jesus used include a prostitute who was about to be stoned, a child who ran away from his father only to return penniless (but was still welcomed), a tax collector, and children. Open the Good Book and read for yourself! It's amazing, those whom God used: Moses, Noah, Abraham, Sarah, Mary, Joseph, Elizabeth, John the Baptist. I recently found out even Jesus's brother didn't believe in Him until a certain point in Jesus's ministry. Is that incredible, or what?

I can remember some of these stories from when I was a kid, and if I dig deep, I can remember how I felt when I first discovered some of these stories. Then, for some reason, the memories are just gone.

Now, as I am teaching my four-year-olds, singing the songs, and personally diving deeper, I find myself drawn more and more into the word.

By diving deeper, I have found out that Jesus was obedient to his Father, humble, passionate, compassionate, self-sacrificing, and vulnerable. He grieved, He blesses us with paradise, He pursues us, He never leaves or forsakes us, He can rule our hearts, and He calls us to bear one another's burdens. Wow ... and that's not even scraping the bottom of the list. That's just a tiny inkling of what he does and what he feels.

As we go through these sermons, I have been making notes and circling my favorite verses along the way. I write them on note cards and leave them on my desk at work. I really need to keep one in my car too so I can constantly remind myself of what the verses are. One of my favorites is Hebrews 12:2 (NIV).

Let us fix our eyes on Jesus, the author and perfecter of our faith, who for the joy set before him endured the cross, scorning its shame, and sat down at the right hand of the throne of God.

Okay, let's look closer at this one: "Let us fix our eyes on Jesus, the author and perfecter of our faith." So, if we keep our eyes fixed on Jesus, He will be the author and perfecter of our faith. All I have to do is read His word, study His word, and keep my eyes on Him, and He will perfect my faith. Wow ... He endured the cross for the joy set before Him. He wanted a relationship with me so badly that He was crucified and died for me. Has anyone on earth endured any pain at my expense to have a relationship with me? Uh, no! No earthly person has endured pain for me and said, "I am suffering for you, so you will have a relationship with me." Not one. Knowing someone was willing to suffer what he suffered, how can I even remotely think I will not be all in for Christ?

I cannot even fathom not being as close to Jesus as He wants to be with me! Like Jesus, I have family who do not believe in me. But I am going to remain in Him. Like the prostitute Jesus saved, there are those who will persecute me. But I will remain in Him. Like the tax collector, there are those who believe I should not be allowed to have a relationship with Jesus. But I will remain in Him. I know people who have burdens, and I will choose to bear those burdens with them, and I will remain in Him. Over the past 31.5 weeks, I have had many people who have poured into me, helped me grown, helped me see who I really am, held my hand, held my heart, carried my burdens when I couldn't, showed me compassion, and showed me real love. These people remain in Him. I find myself constantly amazed when I truly think that someday, those who are hungry will have a feast that never ends, the blind will truly see and find themselves stunned by the glorious colors, the lame will dance because their legs are able to move, and the weary (and I know this from experience) will truly find rest in His arms. I am constantly wanting and craving more of Jesus, more of His words and commands, more of His direction. I am so blessed to know that God wants me, He calls me His creation, and He beckons me closer in such a way I don't comprehend, but I am certainly happy, blessed, humbled, joyful, and excited. I find myself seeing colors more brightly, my steps are lighter, and I feel like dancing all the time. When I am weary and think I cannot go on, I pray, pull His hands tighter around me, and remind myself, "I don't belong here," and until the day I see His face, I'll remain in Him.

## August 1, 2015—The Estranged Daughter Is Getting Married

What is every mom's dream for her daughter? What day does every mom look forward to with a taste that is bittersweet with her daughter? You're right: the wedding day. Since the day my daughter was born, I have been looking forward to the night she comes home to tell me she's engaged and planning an engagement party, a bridal shower, shopping for wedding stuff, shopping for her dress, flowers, and invitations. Then there is the day I get to tell my daughter she looks incredibly beautiful, how I am so proud of the wonderful woman she has become, and how I wish her and her new husband all the best. I was looking forward to seeing his face as she walked down the aisle.

It was recently brought to my attention my one and only child is getting married—October 3, 2015, to be exact. I will not be able to attend obviously because it has been thirty-two weeks since I have seen or heard from her. I will not be able to enjoy any of the mother-daughter bridal stuff that is so incredibly precious.

My heart is broken in so many pieces at this time, and I have no idea how to put it back together.

I'm assuming my parents will assume the role I had been looking forward to. I cannot express how this makes me feel.

All the times we watched *Father of the Bride* together … I will cherish those memories.

My daughter and her fiancé have registered and are picking out kitchen items, bathroom towels, a toaster, and lamps. I looked forward to this day and the excitement to be enjoyed because my daughter had found her perfect match.

I would have gushed over her ring and been so happy to congratulate my future son-in-law and welcome him to our small family.

I would have bought them some sort of a gift to celebrate the engagement, and I would have taken any amount of loan to make her wedding the days of her dreams.

I remember when we would watch *Four Weddings* or *Say Yes to the Dress* together. We would talk about the different weddings and dresses and the amount of money, food, and desserts. I totally enjoyed these moments, and now that is what I'll have to cherish—the moments when we dreamed about her wedding day.

Now, she is not a total girlie girl like me and the froufrou of a wedding day didn't excite her like it did me. But as a mom, this is the day you truly look forward to: your daughter's wedding day, and the birth of her children. I certainly hopes she finds her heart before that day happens!

Yesterday, when I discovered her bridal registry, I was pretty okay. I had felt this day would come, and she would marry way to young—but I always thought we would have reconciled our relationship, and I would be included.

Now, someone else will get to help her get her dress on, pull the veil over her face, hand her the bouquet, and give her words of wisdom. Someone else will take the seat of mother of the bride, light the unity candle, watch her walk down the aisle, hear her say her vows, and hear the minister announce, "Mr. and Mrs. ..." Someone else will watch her enjoy her reception, watch her cut the cake, and maybe share a dance or two. Someone else will pack the presents in the car and drop them off so they can be opened after the honeymoon, and someone else will watch her get into her car and be whisked away for her honeymoon. Someone else will come home to an empty nest without her and wish her to be a baby again. But no matter how sad I am today, no matter what pain I feel and the tears that fall, there is hope in front of me. There is a hand still holding me, and that is the hand of Jesus. He never lets go, and He will continue to walk the dark and the broken places. There is still hope in front of me, and maybe someone will come for me.

## *August 20, 2015—A Memo to the Women Who Believe They Can Take My Place*

> You, therefore, have no excuse, you who pass judgment on someone else, for whatever point you judge another, you are condemning yourself. (Romans 2:1 NIV)

Dear Women,

Yes, this letter is for you. The women believing the stories my daughter has told, without even asking me for my side.

Did you have dreams as a child of becoming a mom?

Did you used to tell your grandma you wanted to marry a doctor and have six children, horses, and dogs?

Did you dream of finding a man who would be just like you—loving, kind, and compassionate?

Did you cry when you heard stories of moms hurting their children and killing them?

Did you carry Aurora in your tummy as first a dream and then a reality?

Did you vomit twenty-four seven for the first twenty-two weeks of her gestation?

Did you cry when you heard her heartbeat for the very first time and laugh when you felt her move?

Did you eat healthier, walk, get plenty of rest, prop your feet up, read to her in your stomach, and tell her how happy you were she was coming for your entire pregnancy?

Were you scared when you were in labor and think about the women who have strokes or die giving birth?

Did you finally relax when the doctor told you they were doing a c-section, and your baby would be here in fifteen minutes or less, adding that you would be fine?

Did you count all her fingers and toes and admire her beautiful face and dark hair?

Did you stay up with her during sleepless nights and rock her when her tummy hurt?

Did you cry when she got her shots as an infant and kiss her spots where the needles entered her tiny legs?

Did you research everything you could before she received her cancer diagnosis?

Did you cry for seven straight days and nights, and cut her curls secretly and put them in an envelope after her cancer diagnosis?

Did you go to the chapel on 7 West and beg the Lord for strength and guidance to see you through this most horrific time in your life?

Did you petition for a cure for leukemia?

Did you spend countless hours working on speeches and speaking in front of people with knees shaking, not because you wanted recognition but because you wanted a cure for this disease that took thirty-two lives as you watched your daughter survive?

Did you place your daughter in the tub with bubbles one night and answer her question, "Is cancer going to make me die?"

Did you feel survivor's guilt because your child lived but others died?

Did you survive on Cheerios for the first six months after you left your first marriage, eating them for breakfast, lunch, and a snack because they were cheap and somewhat fulfilling?

Did you worry while lying awake at night and wonder how you would pay the bills, pay the private school tuition, and buy groceries because your ex didn't pay child support?

Did you question everything you were doing to help yourself make ends meet because others were judging your actions and condemning you without asking you your intentions? Did you watch her struggle with homework, cry when her friends left her, hold her head when she had stomach flus, and cry when she had her wisdom teeth extracted? Did you drive her to school every day of her school career and worry about her maybe getting shot at school, or a fire burning the school down, or a tornado crushing her under the debris from the school? Did you worry about her coming home from school alone some days, or getting kidnapped? Did you pray for her when she had too much homework, too many tests to take, or too many friends to confront? Did you curl her hair for the prom and feel so proud because she was absolutely beautiful in her dress?

Did you plan her sixteenth birthday party only to hear her say she wanted the money to go to charity? Did you keep that donation going until she turned eighteen without her ever knowing?

Did you worry about her having periods from the devil and wonder whether the cancer had somehow messed up her female organs, and she may never have children?

Did you worry about her dating and getting herself in a situation that a boy would harm her in some way?

Did you teach her to drive without help from anyone?

Did you lie in her room with her and listen to countless stories about theater, school, teachers, and friends?

Did you listen to her dreams for her future?

Did you support all her decisions, whether you believed in them or not, because they were her dreams?

Did you worry about her and boyfriends one, two, and three?

Did you rethink every parenting mistake you've made?

Did you apologize when you were wrong?

Did you worry about the parenting decisions you made and wonder whether they were right or wrong?

Did you stand up for her when no one else would?

Did you worry incessantly about her since the day she was born?

Did you cherish every single second you had with her, the good and bad?

Did you worry whether her cancer had come back every time she got sick?

Did you plan for and try to make her senior year as special as you could, adding little surprises along the way?

Did you stay awake at night during her senior year and wonder whether you had prepared her enough for the big world?

Did you worry if her new boyfriend was on the up and up?

Did you cry for four days straight when she left?

Did you stay on your knees for weeks after she left and pray for her return?

Did you scream and cry in agony when you got the change of address card in the mail, and stand in the middle of her bed sobbing?

Did it take all of your power to get out of bed every morning and go to work, and then cry most of the day every day after she left?

Did your boss continuously tell you it was going to be okay and that you must keep going?

Did you go home from work every night for the first twenty-four weeks, hug her dog, and tell her you were sorry her mommy was gone?

Did you beg and plead with every adult who knew where she was for ten weeks to tell you where she was and how she was doing?

Did you file a missing person report, and were you made to feel you were a horrible mom because you're the reason your child ran away?

Did you go to the church and your therapist weekly to seek guidance and counsel to rest, reflect, repent, and reconcile?

Did you beg and plead with people to forgive you of the sins you committed and help you understand the why of what happened?

Did you have your family turn their backs on you and never ask your side of the story because you had a history of childhood sexual abuse, as well as a failed first and second marriage that you couldn't deal with yourself, and now those were being used against you?

Do you have anxiety attacks for the fear you'll never see your daughter again?

Do you keep a journal of your life so if you die before you see her again, she will know what you were doing and how you were feeling?

Do you cry yourself to sleep every night?

Do you continue to seek counsel of your church and therapist so you can learn to deal with the information about your child that hurts to deep to think about?

Do you send her e-mails and beg for reconciliation?

Did you call her mother and ask her mom's side of the story regarding why she believes Aurora left?

Did you check your facts after the stories Aurora told you?

Did you refuse to even speak to Aurora's mom and try to help her reconcile with Aurora?

Did you pray every night for God to soften Aurora's heart and work out life with you?

Do you check your e-mails every morning to see if there is one from her?

Do you save a place at church every Sunday for her?

Do you try to find her in the crowd at the College Age Ministry, hoping she will, like their name, return?

Do you wake up every morning and pray this is the day you see her again?

My belief is you do none of these things. You have not walked in my shoes, carried the scars of her, or tried to mend the pieces that once were together as your heart.

Therefore, remember it is not our place to judge one another. It is our duty to have kindness, compassion, empathy, and love. Therefore, turn back time, be born in my skin, live the life I have lived, and carry the burdens I have carried. Then, and only then, will I allow you to take my place. Until then, I pray for your heart too.

## *September 7, 2015—Owning My Anger*

I find myself angry. There are those who say I need to start my antidepressant again, but surprise to all of you: I was angry before I stopped it. I'm sure others will wonder what I am angry about. I can list a few for you!

1. I have family who know where she is but will not give me one hint as to what my daughter is doing, where she goes, whether she is in school, whether she is alive, what kind of car she drives, and what her cell phone number is. I can go on and on and on this one.

2. I am tired of cooking, cleaning, grocery shopping, and doing nothing but work, work, work. Thank goodness for a few close friends who see my exhaustion and the need to be emotionally recharged from time to time. To you, my most precious girlfriends, I love you more than I can ever mention, and I thank you for your time you invest in me. Your compassion and silent understanding mean the world to me. I know you know who I'm talking about.

3. I am angry because my efforts to reach out to my daughter are fruitless. I can apologize and ask forgiveness; recognize her birthday, holidays, and engagements; and send cards, e-mails, presents, and money. It all goes unrecognized, and certainly no mention of receipt is given.

4. I am angry because I am being treated like I am a drug-seeking, child-beating, POS prostitute who has never done anything to benefit her child. And those who believe her story and never seek me out to

ask anything of me think they are so right, but in all actuality, if we read our Bibles and seek God's counsel, you will see they are clearly wrong. But you can't tell them that, because clearly they think they are without sin. Good for them!

5. I am upset because I have two diseases that are robbing me of my health and causing daily pain, bloating, stomach issues, and toilet issues, and the only one who is taking pains to help is me.

6. I am upset because I am rowing a boat by myself, and all I really want is for someone else to pick up the oars and row for a while. Would that really be so hard?

7. I am angry because every parental mistake I've made has been raked over the coals of those who shouldn't judge, and I have not been given the chance to plead guilty or defend myself. The charges, trial, verdict, and sentence have all been made without the star witness.

8. I am upset because I am tired of praying and being met with not an iota of an answered prayer. I know—all in God's time, and good things come to those who wait, and God is working on it, and He does all things for our good. I would simply appreciate one hint of an answer.

9. I am upset because my daughter has gotten engaged and is planning a wedding without me. Seriously, planning a wedding without me. But my daughter's disdain for me right now is so huge that she will take her vows, someone else will walk her down the aisle, someone else will answer the question "Who gives this woman?" someone else will light the candles, someone else will pull her veil over her face, someone else will give the toast, someone else will help her with dress, someone else will hand her the bouquet, and someone else will watch her give her first kiss as a wife.

10. I am upset that not one person has chosen to give her a dose of reality, as I would if this was someone's child I know, and say, "Hey, wake up. You are slowly killing your mom. You will regret this someday. Give her a chance to show you how her life has changed.

Give her a chance to be forgiven. Give her a chance to show you anything." They should remind her of the fact that I loved her first, I grew her, I birthed her, I prayed for her safety and her dreams, I sacrificed to make her happy, and I will (unlike my family) be here for her no matter what. No matter what, even after all the pain I've been in because of her, I would welcome her home in a heartbeat. I would take all her anger just to hear her voice. I would crawl through fire for her.

11. I am angry because she made my worst nightmare come true. She got mad and walked away, and I know I'll never see her again. All the faith in the world will not change that fact.

12. I am angry that her fiancé and his family claim to be such great Christians, yet they allow this distance to continue.

13. I am angry because I am lonely. I miss her. I miss her so much that I ache sometimes. What do you do without your child who is out there avoiding you, ignoring you, and pretending you don't exist? How does a mom deal with that?

14. I am angry because what I thought would be the "friend" phase of our lives is gone. Just gone.

15. I am angry because people don't understand that family functions make me sad. I don't want to celebrate birthdays and holidays and children's special moments, or sporting events and graduations. Does anyone understand how painful they are? I used to do those things with my daughter, and now they are gone. There is no time limit on this grief, folks. I feel what I feel, and I cannot fake happiness for you or anyone else. I have a hard time faking happiness for myself at times.

16. I am upset with myself because if I found out some members of my family were deceased, I don't know that I would care. I recently talked to someone I am emotionally close to about this, and she has her own issue with a family member. She confided in me she feels the

same way. Does this make us bad people? I am not sure, but I think God sees the pain more than He sees the anger, and He understands.

17. I am upset because after all I've said already, I still just want my daughter to call me, write me, send me a note, and say, "Hey, I'm alive, and I love you. I'm just working through some things, but I recognize all you did for me. I know you did your best, and I know you made mistakes. I love you, Mom."

These are just a few things that have upset me, which is clearly the human side of me. The Christian side says, It will all be okay. You will see her again. You must continue to pray (1 Chronicles 16:11; Romans 8:26). You must continue to persevere (Proverbs 3:5–6; James 1:12). You must continue your journey and rest, reflect, repent, and reconcile. I feel like the little train that could, and I think I can make it one more day. I think I cannot cry one more tear, but I think I can keep the faith (Luke 7:50).

I'm angry for the moment and possibly having a pity party for myself. I think it's okay, and I think those who love me the most will understand. My dogs certainly understand, and I love them so much. They keep me sane these days, Harlie with her snuggling in bed and Jordyn with her never-ending hugs. I will get through this. I will wake up every day and keep going. I will rejoice in the Lord during this time of trial because I know the path is set by Him, and I know His love is perfect, and I know He is walking with me.

God has seen me take ownership for all my sins, mistakes, regrets, and repentance, and I want the chance to show my daughter. But I realize she must give me the chance. I was thinking about our trip to the beach last year and how we laughed and sang and shared quiet moments. That was the best week ever for me. It reminded me of our trip to Clifty Falls, our hikes in the woods, and lying by the pool. Such great memories for me.

I would love the chance to see her again and tell her I love her, I'm sorry for my mistakes, and I would love the time to show her how my life and heart have changed. But again, I'm not the one not reaching out. There is no indication how long the prodigal son was gone. I wish I knew a time table and the hour of her return. I wish I knew I wouldn't be old, gray, and on death's door. Time is so short, so precious. My anger has subsided while writing. Now I'm melancholy. I guess I'll walk the dogs and enjoy the great outdoors, sunshine, and the love of a dog. I will enjoy God's warmth of the sun and His unconditional love from a furry face. Until later, my friends, I leave you with Psalm 51: "Grant me a willing spirit to sustain me."

A willing spirit to sustain me. Lord, how I need this spirit. Daily, I take up my cross of loneliness and keep going. Daily, I cry myself to sleep, wondering where Aurora is and how she is doing, what she is up to, and what her life is like now. The sadness overwhelms me at times, and I know God is with me, but it would be nice to have a human daily to have contact with. I go to my BFF's office and get hugs periodically. The weekly conversations with my therapist help me feel I have a human connection. Lord, keep sustaining me. I need You.

It's hard to express all the emotions that flow through you as a parent estranged from a child. I now know there is a word for it: *estranged*. I'm finding out several people have children they are estranged from, and as parents, none of us truly understand it. I always thought I would be able to talk through any issue I've ever had, but maybe not. Having someone totally cut you off with no explanations and no communication is like a death, but you don't have closure. You mourn, but there is no grave to visit. You grieve, but there is no one to grieve with you because others are still having a relationship with the child. You realize you can be happy, but when you want to share happy moments with your family, there is always that one person you still want to share life with, but you can't. They are out there, but you cannot speak to them. For the time you have estrangement, you continue in the grieving steps: anger, denial, acceptance—pretty big ones for me.

## September 21, 2015—I Surrender All

"I surrender all, I surrender all, all to thee my blessed savior, I surrender all." - Judson W. Van DeVenter and Winfield S. Weeden, "I Surrender All", Published 1896

There is an old hymn I grew up on, and the words go like this "I surrender all, I surrender all, all to thee my blessed savior, I surrender all, humbly at his feet I bow, worldly pleasures all forsaken, make me Savior holy thine, may thy holy spirit fill me, may I know my power divine." I used to love to sing this song in harmony with my dad; his full bass/tenor voice and my alto/soprano voice sounded so pretty in my mind. Recently, I had a church friend talk about surrendering her own estranged child to God. Within a few short days, her child returned home. Oh, how I wish that was my story, but it isn't.

And now, well, it's been another form of labor because it's now been nine months, one day, and twenty-three hours since my daughter left. It's been a very long nine months … but it's also been a good nine months. I know that sounds strange, even to me, to say out loud, to believe out loud, but it's been okay. I'm going to be okay, and eventually she will be okay. Because I surrender all …

I finally surrendered and have changed her room to be what I want a girlie room to look like. I sleep better in that room than I do anywhere else in the house. I read my Bible more because I am spending time with the one thing that loves me and knows I am worth more than anyone else does. I see my therapist once a week and get my toes done every other week; it's the one time I get undivided human interaction and human touch without any complaining or feelings of guilt because I took people away from their phones, work, or families.

I surrendered my feelings of being unworthy, expanded my friend horizon, and spent more time with a woman I have something in common with: twice divorced, and an estranged family.

I've surrendered to my feelings of shame and learned if you have a problem with those who say they are Christians, but they treat you in a non-Christian like way, maybe they have a problem, not you. I've also surrendered I am not the only sinner, and I learned that we as sinners all fall short of the glory of God, but only a few select few can admit this and be aware to the fact that we all do sin.

I've surrendered my feelings of guilt and learned you can be the best mother you know how to be, and your children will still find fault with you and walk away. I've learned sometimes a child comes back in two weeks, two months, two years, seven years, and, the most recent, ten years.

I've learned my job as a mom is to continue to love, support, and pray for my daughter's heart no matter how she treats me. I've learned some members of my family have some serious issues that don't involve me because I've done my part of rest, reflect, and repent, and I can only own my part in a relationship.

I've learned to forgive my family, my daughter, her boyfriend, his family, and all the other adults who say, "I don't want to be involved," but clearly are because they chose a side. I'm surrendering their hearts to God; only He can open their hearts, not me.

I've surrendered myself to God and learned to forgive myself for my shortcomings and to know it's okay to be human; we all are, and we all make mistakes.

I've learned to pray for everyone involved, including myself.

I've surrendered to the fact I am truly nothing without God and His glorious Son, who came to forgive me for all my sins, who made me fearlessly and wonderfully, and who just wants my heart. I turned to Him, and He ran to me, which is exactly what I'll do when my daughter decides she has forgiven me and wants to reconcile.

I have surrendered to a God who has always loved unconditionally and who makes all things new. I have surrendered to my brothers and sisters in Christ; their blood runs thicker than any earthly family's blood could ever run.

I have surrendered and now invest in others—not on Facebook, Twitter, Myspace, or Instagram, but real, face-to-face conversations with people. I pour my heart into them, and it means much more than any Facebook post. I have learned I have a huge heart and huge ears, and my shoulders can handle more weight with the love of Jesus helping to support.

I surrender to the reality I may not have my daughter; she is following her own path, finding her own way, and living her own journey. But I have more people investing in me, keeping me from turning away from God in pain, and encouraging me to lean on Him in an authentic, "He loves me no matter what" type of way.

I've surrendered my pain to God. He is the only one who can heal it. My parents can't admit my pain because they would have to look at themselves and see their piece in this puzzle. My sister can't admit my pain because she would have to admit she was wrong in sending me a nasty text message. My aunt and cousin can't because they would have to turn to themselves. My daughter, for the moment, can't because for her to admit she caused me pain, she would have to admit she was part of the pain. For whatever reason, she cannot admit her part. I surrender her heart to God. He will heal her pain, as He is healing mine. He will open her eyes and let her see she has a mom who loves her unconditionally and will do whatever needs to be done so we can continue the relationship God wants us to have.

I am fully aware of my shortcomings. I have discovered my flaws, I have owned my part, and I have forgiven myself. I surrendered my life to Christ in June. I cannot do this on my own, and it's been through the grace and mercy and loving arms of those I have been walking with that I can stand here today. These people prayed for me to surrender my story to the Lord, and I did. The day I did so, I felt a freedom I've never felt.

Sure, I will make mistakes, I will fall short, I will fail God, I will hurt people unintentionally, and I will shame myself in the future. I'm not perfect, and I will not be perfect until I reach heaven's gates. Saying I'm proud of who I am right now sounds a little snooty, and I don't like to be snooty, but I will say I am truly pleased and honored and humbled to be called a child of God. He loves me and feels I am worthy. I was lost and I found Him, and He ran to me, wrapped his arms around me, and said, "Welcome home, child." I am a princess because my Father is the King of kings. I have a wonderful family in Christ. I am blessed, worthy, and loved. I have surrendered my life, and although this path is lonely at times, all I have to do is look to the heavens and see the stars, the moon, the sun, and the clouds, and I don't feel so lonely anymore. I have surrendered to the one with all the power who loves me and will never let me fall.

I surrender my life, my heart, and my devotion to the one true king, to the one who loves all, knows all, and is all. I surrender. Surrender means to relinquish control or possession of something.

> The Lord gives strength to his people the Lord blesses his people with peace. (Psalm 29:11 NIV)
>
> Now to him who is able to do immeasurably more than all we ask or imagine, according to his power that is at work within us. (Ephesians 3:20 NIV)
>
> From him the whole body, joined and held together by every supporting ligament, grows and builds itself up in love, as each part does its work. (Ephesians 4:16 NIV)

## *October 3, 2015—My Freeway Table Group*

I've been doing this really cool Bible study at church called Freeway. It's produced by the People of the Second Chance, and you should go to their website and check them out. It's so incredibly powerful, and at the end of the sermon series of Freeway, our music minister sang a song by Big Daddy Weave called "My Story." The song tells of a person who was hopeless but found hope, who was loved but didn't love, and who had a life that did not make sense. The person was in the depth of despair but, because of God's grace, was reconciled to Him. The person could live because God lives in him.

This series told our stories of addictions, infidelity, chronic pain, prodigal children, misguided childhoods, sexual abuse, the question of divorce, and the sufferings of being apart from our earthly families.

But this is not where our story ends. Our stories continue into the world to share, to learn from, to overcome, and to declare to Satan that he will not win. Victory belongs to Jesus, our Lord and Savior and the one to who all glory and honor is forever.

Whether we backpedal into old habits; file for divorce; fight for our marriage; cry to God in pain, in our sufferings, or in our joys; or relieve painful pasts, our freedom is through Christ and Christ alone. Our freeway is to share our story and show others who are suffering that through His grace that they too can find freedom. Our freeway is through the blood, the tears, and the sacrifices. It is by picking up our cross daily, taking the hand of Jesus, and walking with Him and living with Him. In Him and through Him, we will be a light unto the world to pave the freeway for those with whom we walk.

It has been a truly humbling experience to share my story of my daughter and my earthly family's betrayal, and to learn I am not the only broken human walking the earth. I thank my table group from the bottom of my being for taking the time to go through what seemed to be such a simple book but turned into a heart-wrenching, joy-filled experience of being prodigal myself, becoming aware of what I needed to change, discovering how I can improve, owning what I need to own, forgiving others, and most important forgiving myself. I have learned to accept and love who I am because God made me, and I am worthy. I encourage you to find your freeway. It's empowering, difficult, thought-provoking, and extremely difficult as you learn to discover, own, accept, and love yourself. More important, it's freeing to discover a love that no earthly human can ever extend to you. If you need me, I'll be on the freeway. Love and hugs to you all!

## *October 13, 2015—Finding Home*

The mind governed by the flesh is death, but the mind governed by the Spirit is life and peace. (Romans 8:6 NIV)

A few years ago, I truly lost my way. I thought I knew which way I was headed. I was stuck in life. Of course, this was by my own choosing because I was ignoring the call of the greater power. I was exhibiting freewill. Yes, things were terribly wrong and I was not happy, but I was too afraid to make changes.

So many times, we see something wrong with our own lives, but instead of having the courage to change, we wait for someone else to do the changing, so we spend a lifetime in misery. I am here to say I am no longer stuck, and I finally found the courage to make the changes I should have made years ago.

I could sit here and say I don't know how it happened, things "just happened," I "didn't see it coming," or "I thought things were going to get better." That's simply not true. Sometimes the truth is in front of you, but you refuse to see it.

Every action I committed played a part in bringing me to where I was. But I'm not there anymore—I saw the truth, I felt the truth, and I am living truth.

I used to think I was too far away to be saved so I should just be thankful I was floating above water with a tiny oar all my own, and it was too late for me to turn things around. Thankfully, I am not there anymore. I found my oar, I found my peace, and I found my voice to say, "No more."

I am truly thankful for those who walked alongside in silence, waited for me to find grace, spoke the truth to me in love, and gently prodded me to truth. I'm extremely indebted to those who showed me the error of my ways and waited patiently for me to catch up, face my fears, not stay in the dark, and come toward the light.

Life seems so much brighter now. The sky seems bluer, the rain is not as gray, the grass is definitely greener, the birds sing louder, and I feel lighter!

I finally found home. Home is not a house, it is not living with people, and it is not laundry, cooking, cleaning, or refilling toilet paper rolls.

Home is in the arms of a Savior who sees all of me and loves me just as I am. Home is being comfortable in the muck and knowing you're not alone. Home is the security of facing your giants and conquering them! I am here to face them, to slay them; I have my slingshot, and I have my stone!

I will never be perfect, but I am loved by one who most certainly is perfect! I believe I was put on earth for a purpose. I am here to be a fisher of men and women, to help the broken, the wounded, the hurt, and the ones who feel worthless. I am here to feel, to love, to care, to show kindness, to empathize, to sympathize, and to show people their lives too can be full of God's wonderful grace.

There are life-changing moments we all have. There is the one aha moment, as Kyle Idleman so eloquently writes about in his book. There is the one morning you wake up and realize you are worth more than the life you are living. I am so overwhelmed by the steps of confronting, condemning, and the courage I have been given through our Lord and Savior. His wonderful mercy and grace have proven to be my best friend. It was always there; I simply needed to see it, to reach for it, to rest in it and in Him. I remain in Him …

If you think you are stuck, if you think you cannot come home, or if you think you're too far away, hang tight and grab this oar, because like me, you never are!

I was beginning to see how all my mistakes changed me, and how they affected my family and friends. I heard so many times, "We don't know what really happened in your home; only God really knows," that I didn't like hearing that sentence. It took on a meaning at the time I didn't understand. It made me angry, and at first I was angry at others. Then I realized the only person I had to be angry with was myself. I made the choices and decisions, and it is up to me to suffer the most severe consequences of those actions. The first step was to forgive myself, and I could do that only with God's help.

# *November 11, 2015—There Is a War between Guilt and Grace*

---

"I'm a mess and so are you, we've built walls nobody can get through." —Francesca Battistelli

---

There is a war between guilt and grace. There is a war between sinners and saints. There is war between being who Christ wants us to be and who our earthly families project us to be. There is war between letting go of your past and realizing you are a new creation in Christ and extending true forgiveness. I am quickly learning this is not so easy for many people. At times, I'm at a loss as to what to do with that information.

I realize I made mistakes in my past, and I realize I've hurt others. I'm not asking for the past to be erased, but when you have truly asked forgiveness and apologized for your wrongdoings, why is that so hard for humans to let go of? I thank my Lord and Savior hourly at times for His mercy and grace. If not for Him, I truly don't know where I would be. I've learned it is truly only through Him we are made new, and it is only through those truly walking with Him that grace, mercy, and forgiveness are extended.

My life has taken several turns and twists over the past five years. Most recently, the changes God has bestowed upon me are those that completely overwhelm me at times. I gave my life back to Him in June. I quit trying to fix things and stayed in constant prayer over what He wanted for my life. I then remained silent and listened. And listened. And listened. When we remove ourselves from life, we get a clear indication from Him as to where He is leading us. When I listened, I found a whole new joy and a completely different life from what I thought I wanted for me. I found happiness, love, peace, and understanding. How freeing has this been? I must tell you, once I removed me from me, life became worth living again.

I am not saying life is perfect. Can life on earth be perfect? I don't know, but it sure feels better than it has before. Francesca Battistelli sings a song called "If We're Honest." I listened to this song maybe a thousand times, and her lines about "truth is harder than a lie" and "don't pretend you're something that you're not, living life afraid of getting caught" touched a nerve for me. I realized this is exactly what I had been doing: pretending I was something to gain love. The life I was living wasn't happy; it was full of stress, turmoil, and constant struggle. Once I gave my life to God and realized He had something greater in store for me, I began to let go of the pretending and was led to the real friendships and relationships I was craving. Oh, sure, in the beginning of the letting go process, I was sad and torn, but then I realized I had given my life to God, and that's what mattered most. No human will fill the void and give you the love God does. Look at what He did for us. He gave His only Son to die on the cross for our sins. Jesus took the suffering of the entire world on just so we would have a relationship with His Father. If we remain in Him, He remains in us. That kind of love isn't found anywhere on earth—or on any other planet, for that matter!

I was recently told that I needed to be ready to suffer like Jesus did on the cross for my mistakes and the pain that I have caused. Well, in actuality, Christ already suffered for me. All I need to do is listen to those I have hurt, apologize, and ask forgiveness. I have already suffered at the loss of my daughter. I have written, called, and e-mailed, and I have apologized over and over again for whatever it is I did to hurt her. I truly am sorry. No one but God can see the pain in my heart for knowing I hurt her. It was not intentional; I am human, and I was going through my own junk and had to take my own journey to redemption.

And so I've given up the war between guilt and grace. I am letting God's grace win. I will not let myself be torn by Satan and continue to beat myself up for my past. I will not allow anyone working in Satan's court drag me down and turn me into what they want me to be. My one and only goal on earth is to walk where God wants me to walk, love those He puts in my path, rejoice with my fellow brothers and sisters in Christ, and receive all the love they bestow upon me. My joy is found in Him. There is a comfort in suffering in Him. He knows my heart; He sees me as His child. For those who want to put me in their world and see me only through their eyes, I'm sorry for them. I will pray for them. When we open our hearts and eyes and see people as Christ sees them, all we will know is the extension of grace and love. God will always plead our course and right our wrongs. He gave His life so we could have ours. In His eyes, there is only grace. He breaks all our chains, and He overcame. He says we are free! I'm going to stay free and remain in His love.

## *November 15, 2015—Love*

Love really is a beautiful thing, is it not? And isn't real, true love that much better? I just finished reading Gary Chapman's *Five Love Languages* and certainly have a better understanding of myself now. I am definitely an "act of service" and "words of affirmation" kind of girl. I didn't realize this a few years ago, but this past year has been all about self-discovery. My life hasn't been ideal for a while, but over the past six months, I've reached out, learned, and explored, and I have a truly better understanding of myself and what I want out of life.

Oh, yes, I've been accused of several different things over the past few weeks, but as my counselor and I talked, those who can't see me for me are dealing with their own pain and their own junk. If they blame me for their wrongs, well, that makes them feel better, and I can live with that because I used to do the same thing—blame others for my shortcomings and the things that were wrong in my life. It helps in the short term and certainly allows you to be angry about things, but in the end, is being angry and blaming others really the way to go? I would say not, but as a former angry blamer, I'll allow the hurt to come my way.

As I said recently, I was told that I need to "suffer like Jesus did on the cross" for my sins and past transgressions. That sentence made me realize I was dealing with people who want to stay in the past, who want to dwell on my mistakes, my sins, and my failures. Okay, you stay there. As for me, I'm moving forward. I'm letting go. I'm moving toward a better, positive beginning.

I'm in my own personal battle now, a fight to get my daughter back, a quest to make her life and mine better than it's ever been. It started with me finally taking care of me. It all started with me realizing first and foremost I am the child of the one true King, and He loves me for me, and He will do anything to keep me in His life, including forgiving my sins and allowing me to move forward with my life. In that quest, I have tried to let go of some relationships that I felt were dragging me down. Evidently they were, because for the past two weeks, I have found myself sleeping sounder, losing more weight, and feeling lighter in every aspect of my life. I am laughing more and crying less, and people have told me I am glowing. Now, I know for sure I am not expecting a baby, and that's what people usually say about expectant mothers. I am happy about this statement because I know I am truly happy.

I've also been accused of ignoring. It really wasn't an intentional ignore; it just sort of happened. I realized if I reached out and talked, I would be dragged into the same hole of blaming me for what went wrong, for moving forward, and for changing. Okay, I realize it all, but I had to do it for me. Although I want to talk, and although I realize I need to listen to the closure some people need, it won't change who I am now. I can't allow it to change me. You see, all the relationships I have let go of were bad for me. I was searching, loving, hoping, and resting in things that will never change. I was living in the past and holding on to love in the hopes I would get something back. But then I realized the love once there wasn't there anymore. My expectations were too high, and my need for something more was too expensive. The price of the new me meant others hand to change and grow with me. Others have to let go of their own junk and rest in the knowledge that we are all seeking for love that's unobtainable here on earth—not if we continue to pursue love with those who are not found in Christ. Only through Christ and learning what love, forgiveness, patience, faith, mercy, and grace are can we truly love.

And yes, I realize all this sounds like I am a Jesus freak. And that's okay; you can call me that. I am not ashamed that I finally found what it was I was looking for" true forgiveness, grace, mercy. and love that can only be found in Him. No one on earth can grant that, and I finally realize that now. I was wishing for things on earth that cannot be found here. I have found new friends who know about me and chose not to judge me or persecute me. They have taken me in, washed away my sins, and shown me compassion, love, and acceptance. These are all the things everyone else says they do, but if they truly did, when I say, "The past is the past, it needs to stay there, and we need to move forward," they would say, "Yes, I agree. Let's move forward in the grace God grants us all. Let me grow and change with you so our lives can be better and greater than they ever have been before."

I've been told people of my past love me and would do anything of me. It's funny. Where were those people over the past forty-seven weeks? Did they check on me weekly? Did they ever call and say, "Hey, I was thinking about you. Let's do lunch, let's get coffee, let's pray"? Nope, not a one. But I have found my new circle of friends, and we support each other through prayer, texts, e-mails, and phone calls. What's a phone call, you say? It's this thing where you call and speak to someone, and then if needed, you can pray at the end in support of that person's life.

So here I am on my quest to get Aurora back and to let her know that I love her, I accept her for her journey, I want to be a part of her life, and I want to love her with this newfound love that I know I can truly extend—no questions, no fear, and no holding back. But of course, this may not happen until she is out of the home she is living in now. The people she is with now want to live in the past. They want to put me on the cross every time I talk to them, and that I just can't do. Jesus already died for my sins and paid my debt. It's my job now to ask for forgiveness and move forward. This is another group I must let go of. I can't allow myself to continue to be verbally beat up, because people can't move forward.

I miss Aurora every day. I pray for her and her fiancé, and I hope someday she will see me for me and realize I am not the same mom she left. I am stronger, more patient, more forgiving, less willing to let people walk over me, and ready to move forward in a life with Christ.

So here I sit in my home, looking across the woods, watching my friend outside with her kids doing yard work, her husband on the riding lawn mower, the dogs playing together, the leaves falling from the trees. I am hoping and praying Aurora can hear my heart. I am hoping she can feel my prayers. I am keeping the faith that she senses the love coming through the universe and whispering to her heart that I love her, I need her, and I long to be with her.

Every day, every hour, every minute, and every second, I grieve for my daughter and the life we had. It wasn't perfect and it wasn't extravagant, but it was ours, and I know as the adult, I made some decisions and asked people into our lives that I shouldn't have. I never should have married the second time; I shouldn't have had the roommate I had. Those mistakes cost me the only thing I loved and adored. It cost me a huge part of my heart that will never be healed because you can't mourn those who are gone from your life but who are still living. If she had died, people would have sent flowers and brought me a casserole. There would have been a service, and we could have shared our memories and had one important element: closure. Missing the living is an open wound that never heals; sometimes it festers, and you can put a Band-Aid on it, but that is temporary. This wound will heal for a while and then reopens to the pain again.

## November 25, 2015—Giving Thanks

Therefore, since we have been justified through faith, we have peace with God through our Lord Jesus Christ, through whom we have gained access by faith into this grace in which we now stand. And we boast in the hope of the glory of God. Not only so, but we also glory in our sufferings, because we know that suffering produces perseverance; perseverance, character; and character, hope. And hope does not put us to shame, because God's love has been poured out into our hearts through the Holy Spirit, who has been given to us. (Romans 5:1–5 NIV)

Here we are. Another year has come and gone, and even during the midst of a great stormy year, I have abundant blessings, Gad you asked me a year ago if my life would change this much, I would have said no, and I would not have said I was perfectly happy in my current state. But Aurora leaving and pushing me closer to God and out of my comfort zone has been the greatest blessing of all. I found my voice, my heart, my purpose, and my life over the past year, and for that I am very thankful.

I have joined two groups at church and grown more in the past year than I have in the forty-seven years God has given me on this earth. I am happier, have the will to be more open and honest with myself and others, and have learned to lay all my secrets, shame, despair, and joy at the foot of the cross to move forward with life.

I have said goodbye to past hurts, let go of what I cannot change, and learned I am worthy of much more respect, compassion, and love than I have ever let in—and I am thoroughly ready to experience it full force.

I have talked about my first ex-husband and abuse I suffered as a child, and I learned others have walked the same path. The stories may be different, but the outcome is the same: feelings of being unworthy and shamed; feelings of letting down your spouse, your family, and more important God. I have learned there are other women and men out there who have suffered at the hands of loved ones, strangers, and the greatest enemy of all—ourselves.

I have learned it's okay to have a missing child. We are not given a handbook at the birth of our children and told how to deal with every situation in the perfect manner so as to not hurt them with baggage from our pasts and stressful situations in which we find ourselves. This knowledge has helped me forgive my own parents for what I feel are their mistakes and move forward to only want to love them and spend whatever time they have on earth enjoying their presence.

I have learned I do not have to stay in relationships that are stuck in what was and what could be, where I may be the only person working toward a goal of good communication, respect, and commitment to a better future.

I have learned it is okay to stand up for myself and state what I do and do not like about my life. I am within my rights as a human being to have my own opinions, thoughts, and wishes for my life. I do not have to live for everyone else; I can live for me.

I have learned it's okay to be a "Jesus freak," as I have recently been called. He carried me through this past year and never left my side. He spoke to me through friends and family and told me, "I have you." When I asked, He gave me answers to some of life's toughest questions, He gave me the strength to deal with the pain and the tears, and He reconciled my heart to know it's okay to not be okay at times.

I have learned when you are walking with those who truly love you, your pain becomes their pain, and in times of deepest sorrow, your pain is carried by them. When you are healing, you are able to help carry the pain of others.

I have learned there are people who will stick up for you when you are attacked and will fight for your dignity and honor.

I have learned sometimes people truly are put in your life for a season, and it's okay to let them go when the season has ended, wish them well, pray for their happiness, and know you served a purpose for them too.

I have learned God doesn't promise us life will be easy. He promises us that when everything around us is falling, we are held.

I have been blessed, as I stated earlier, with several new friends, and I am enjoying celebrating their blessings: new babies, IVF treatments, job successes, pregnancies—the list is long and joyous.

I have been blessed with love from people I never imagined possible. Love from the past; love with hope for a wonderful future; love with no conditions, no boundaries, no expectations, and no limitations; love full of respect and compassion; love as Christ intended love to be.

As I face this Thanksgiving season without my daughter, I have a lot to be thankful for, and I am so humbled and overwhelmed. I will miss her face and her hugs, and I will miss watching *National Lampoon's Christmas Vacation* after eating our Thanksgiving meal. But that is the short term. If I look to my blessings, I have a wonderful employer and his wife (my friend) whom I will be spending the day with. I have love in my heart. I have a new house waiting for me to make it my home. I have friends who love me for me and see Him in me. I have two dogs who touch my heart with their wagging tails. Does the list end? No, because in Christ I have a brand-new life waiting for me to embrace it, and I couldn't be happier to have a peaceful heart, a humbled spirit, and a renewing of my life. Blessings, my friends.

# December 3, 2015—Heartbeats

As I sit to write tonight, I have no title. I really have no words to even explain what's in my heart. I am going to shoot from the hip here, so bear with me. I have been trying to rebuild a relationship with my family and thought we were making progress, but then this past Tuesday, I received a call from a friend, whose friend called her to let her know a small incident that happened at the hair salon. It seems one of my family members was getting her hair done the same time as my friend's friend, who obviously knew that was a member of my family. It seems this family member was speaking ill of me and stating what a horrible person I was—in public, with other people around. I guess the lady who does my friend's friend's hair knew more about me and my life than she cared to know. This happened less than two weeks ago. How can that be?

Then I got to thinking about my friend who called me to tell me all this, as well as the love I have in my heart for her. She would never lie to me; she would never intentionally do a thing to hurt me. Yet when I asked for things to change in our relationship, she could not love me enough to do so.

That brought me to thinking about my family again. How can you call yourself a Christian and say to my face you love me, yet you turn your back against me?

I've come to the conclusion that humans are incapable of real love if they are not in Christ at all times. It's something I've learned over the past year: to truly love, to truly forgive, to truly be, you have to have Christ in your life. Now, I'm not saying I'm always this perfect person, but I've been completely honest with my feelings on a lot of issues, how I feel about certain things, and what I am capable of as a human.

I've told my family I want the past in the past, and I want us all to move forward in Christ. They say that's what they want too, yet less than two weeks ago, they were at a hair salon talking about how horrible I am. What's with that? My friend was even upset because she doesn't believe the feelings I had at a time in the past for her were real and true. Did I say them just to say them? No, I meant every word of them, but like my relationship with my family, my life has changed drastically in a year's time. I've grown and I've changed. I've realized what's holding me together twenty-four seven. I have to respect that … and more than any human, it's been God holding me together. It's been prayer. It's been a true reflection on God and all He has done for me to get me here. And as I thought about all this and how hard it is to explain to people, I decided to take time and do the four Rs.

What are the four Rs? It's what my daughter's college-age pastor told me to do when she left: rest, reflect, repent, and reconcile. Here's what I've learned about that. I can rest and think about all I've done wrong, and I can beat myself up for it, and I can be sad and think horrible things about myself. I can say I'm sorry for all the hurts I've caused, and then I can try to reconcile relationships. That is what I've been trying to do for almost an entire year now. What I've learned about reconciliation is it cannot happen unless both parties in a relationship are willing to admit hurts, apologize for them, get out of the hurt, and move forward.

So I spent a few hours crying and beating myself up for all the hurt again, and I thought about what I've done over the past eight weeks. I did what every person does in times of need: I e-mailed my DC Chicks and asked for prayer. What I got in return was prayer, phone calls, cyber hugs, and reassurance I am okay and am on the right path. I am learning to let my heart beat again, I am saying goodbye to where I've been, and I am looking at my shattered life that's in about a thousand pieces on the floor. I've been on my knees again, asking God to give me the strength to give up my family, my loves, and my hurts, and to help me realize I don't live in the past but live in the now. I have a future, I have plans, and I have to take one step at a time out of darkness, putting Band-Aids on my scars yet looking at them and appreciating them for what they are: failures. Where I used to be was not a good place. It was a place where I lived for everyone else and didn't do a very good job of it. It was where I was dishonest with myself, and tried to be what everyone else wanted, and wasn't true to myself. It was living but not breathing. It's hard to explain this to anyone who doesn't realize the childhood I had, the marriages I've survived, and the deep pain that existed in my heart. Yesterday is a closed door, and I do not live there anymore. I have to remember first and foremost I'm God's child. He loves me, and this is the season He decided to give His only Son to have a relationship with me, to have me in His love and embrace. My heart is beating, but every now and again, I get pulled into yesterday and want to live in the hurt. I have to say goodbye to the hurt. When you hurt, you hurt others, and I don't want to be the person who hurts others. I don't want to be the one who doesn't let others live to their full potential and get all the wonderful things in life they deserve. So not only do I want my heart to breathe, but I want theirs to breathe too. I think sometimes that means you give up what you love, because by loving it, you cause it more pain. Maybe this makes sense; maybe it doesn't.

Sometimes when I let myself open doors I should leave closed, I live in the hurt. I see the pieces on the floor and realize I'm shattered and have shattered others. I realize I can't put anyone else together unless I put myself together first. And I'm doing that. I'm leaving darkness and reaching for the Son. And for those whom I've hurt, for those whom I've shattered, for those who can't see my heart today: I am sorry. I hope you heal, I hope you find your peace, and I hope you know my heart beats a little for you every day with hope, faith, and longing for a time of reconciliation and healing. I hope someday your heart will also beat again, and I guess that's what this title should be: Heartbeats.

## December 5, 2015—Sisters in Love

---

"I wouldn't choose me first if I was looking for a champion, in fact I'd understand if you picked everyone before me, but that's just not my story." — Francesca Battistelli, "He Knows My Name"

---

Last night, I was able to attend a women's Christmas tea at church. The men served us dressed in black pants and white shirts, and it was the first time in a long time this lady had someone waiting on her. I ate before I went because the Celiac disease keeps me from really participating in meals, but the atmosphere and the conversation beforehand was great. My new friend from DC and I sat together, and her husband was working different tables. As we sat and watched, she told me a little about her insecurities when they first met and how her story affects her relationships now. That was very sweet because I am currently struggling with knowing I am loved, or maybe I should say knowing I am worthy of love. It's a daily struggle for me, and I constantly remind myself that I am worthy.

I then had an opportunity to explore the relationships I've had in the past, and I talked to her about how if people are really nice to me, I have a problem because I don't know nice for the sake of nice. I look at good people in my life and wonder, "Why did God place them here? What do they want, and when will they leave?"

She asked me, "Why wouldn't He?" We then talked about self-worth and how differently we look at things because of our past. I'm used to abuse and negativity, so positive affirmations seem quite odd to me for the moment. I got to thinking about this song one of my other friends loves, "He Knows My Name" by Francesca Battistelli. Then it hit me! Why am I not allowing myself the good? My normal isn't good, and that's why. But over the past few months. I've worked really hard to change my normal, so why not keep embracing it? I lose sight of all the good when I let my past creep into my present. and if I keep doing that, I'll ruin my future.

Another DC friend answered my very long e-mail and suggested that by ignoring my family and choosing to be silent, I am actually allowing myself to heal even more, to keep forgiving, and keep the anger that may creep in at bay. That's being more Christian and helpful than allowing myself to keep begging for the kind of relationship I long for with them but that they are not capable of at the time.

I had to let this simmer for a bit, and I took myself for a pedicure and manicure. I read a little bit of the Bible (I always go to Romans for comfort) and thought about my friend asking me if I wanted her to stand with me when the speaker last night called for those with broken relationships to stand. I truly didn't want to stand, but her encouragement and smile said, "It's all going to be okay. I am here with you." And she was right. Standing and showing the room full of other women that I too have a broken heart, a broken relationship, and a heart that is healing and resting in the arms of our Savior was another step toward healing.

I've handled so much of my life on my own because it was "too much trouble" for anyone to lock arms, or "I have no clue what you're going through, so I'm just going to remove myself from this problem, ignore it, and not mention it, and it will somehow go away." Well, that doesn't happen. All that does is build resentment toward people and make you feel like people don't really care about what you're going through.

For those I've ever done that to, I'm sorry. I truly care about your problems and your sadness, so please forgive me my trespass.

Then on the way to my favorite coffee shop with one of my favorite people, I saw my daughter's BFF—or who used to be her BFF; I have no idea whether or not they are still friends. I have to tell you, she did not look so good, and it was an awkward conversation. After all I've heard my daughter has supposedly said about me, I'm sure she was thinking, "Why is this crazy lady talking to me?" But I embraced it, and hopefully she has told my daughter I saw her and looked happy, because I am.

I'm totally getting off track here. Oops!

Then the speaker started talking about our story: who is the author, what's the beginning, who are the characters, how it ends. My story begins and ends with Jesus. He created me, He perfected me, and He saw the strength He would instill in me to survive child abuse, abusive marriages, and my daughter running away. He gave me the brain to think about what's right and wrong and what steps I need to take to make life better. He has given me the hope that if I remain in Him and He remains in me, I can conquer any giant that comes my way. I am ready to do so, so I'm definitely letting go, again, of past mistakes and negativity in my head. I know it'll be a daily fight until the negativity is gone and all the positive thinking is back. I'm going to remember I am a child of His, and He has me. I'll call on my friends and family in Christ and remember they are the hands of God, and they will lift me up, because on my own, it's not enough. I know they'll have the words of wisdom and hugs and love that I need when I need it most. They are part of my story, and they are the characters. My ending isn't near yet, but I'll keep you posted on the middle. It's going to be great!

# December 20, 2015—Anniversary and Faith

"To learn strong faith is to endure great trials. I have learned my faith by standing firm amid severe testing." —George Mueller

What a great quote for this weekend. Yes, I have seen many trials, and I have learned faith can see you through any storm. This weekend marks the one-year anniversary since my daughter "left home." I have no idea how to word it. Did she run away? Did she leave for a reason? I know she got mad, and instead of choosing to talk about it and be open and honest with me, she left. Has she spoken to me yet? No, but I did get one e-mail in twelve months. Wow, I'm enlightened—not. In turn, members of my family turned their backs on me instead of talking.

What I have learned is maybe this was all for the best. I have learned I tended to surround myself with toxic relationships. No one but my daughter and I are to blame for her leaving, although there were certain factors about my life I could have changed to prevent this from happening. When my parents and I went to counseling a few months ago, and my mom said, "Do you have any idea what we've been through with her?" to my therapist, it hit me. Sometimes parents have issues they haven't dealt with, and even though you say you are a Christian and go to church, sometimes you are not a true follower of Christ. Therefore, you can't let go of your own past hurts, and those demons will soon consume you. I let my demons consume me for many years, and at times they still creep in if I let them, taking over my head sometimes for an entire day. But I will not allow them to define me. I am worth so much more to my Father in heaven than any earthly being could ever understand. I am not going to let anyone who doesn't understand this newfound worth destroy me. It has certainly been used against me in the recent weeks. My happiness and peaceful heart isn't out of the need to rid myself of bad things; it's been used to truly find out who I am, who I want to be, in whom I put my trust, and who sees me for me and not what they want me to be. I used to always put my trust in earthly beings, and I felt if I was just this much better or this thin, or if I thought this way or did this to please others, I would be happy. After Aurora left and my family distanced themselves and wouldn't speak to me, I found myself (with the exception of a few moments where people were there) praying more, listening deeper to Christian songs, looking up the verses in the Bible where the songs came from, and finding a deeper meaning to my hurt. I found that, yes, I had been through some pretty traumatic events in my life, but I was still standing, and the reason is because God had me.

God continues to carry me. Yes, I am happier now at this moment than I believe I've ever been in my life. And even though this weekend was met with four bouts of crying and reaching out to those who have truly walked alongside me during this past year, the e-mails or texts back were full of encouragement, hope, and verses from the Bible I have read several times but continue to speak to my heart.

Now, is it a good thing that my daughter and I are separated, and that even though I continually reach out, she chooses to ignore? No, it's a very sad, hurtful thing. But when she comes back, will I say to her or anyone in the room, "Do you know what I have been through with her?" No. I will simply wrap my arms around her and welcome her back into the place of my heart she belongs. Will I ever blame her for leaving and for the hurt she put me through? No, because if she is anything like me, she already knows what she has done has been extremely painful. It's not my place to make her feel worse; it's my place to make her feel loved. It's what several people have done for me—no judging, no blaming, no condemnation, no words of making her feel worse for the wear. She will feel only love. It's what we are all called to do: rest, reflect, repent, and reconcile. I understand I played a part in her leaving. I understand I did things that hurt her. I understand I was not, and am not, and never will be a perfect mother. But am I forgiven by God, and am I granted grace by God? Yes. It's too bad that earthy beings don't fully grasp the grace God has given us. I think if we all understood this, the world would be a much happier place. Is it easy to extend grace? Not always. Is it healthy for us to do? Yes. And for those who throw my happiness in my face and continue to repeat hurtful comments to me: you do have a place in my heart, and you do have a place in my life, but you have to come to chapter of the book I am in to fully understand my life now. You are not some distant memory, and you are not forgotten, but I cannot and will not continue to live my life in the past. I need my future, and my future will be one of hope, faith, and encouragement, with no judgment or condemnation. I have the extension of true grace. This is something that cannot be explained; it must be experienced. When you walk through the fire and know that God has you, you'll understand. As for me, I'll continue to remain hopeful my daughter will be experience this same aha moment I had earlier this spring and summer. I hope that she'll see me as a parent who made mistakes but loves her child with all her heart. I'll continue to walk in faith, and I will continue to pray for hearts to soften and for people to see me through the eyes of Christ and not their own eyes. For it is only when we see people through Christ's eyes that we can fully extend forgiveness and grace. I'll make it through today because I'm holding strong to faith that endures.

When I say I made mistakes, I'm not talking small mistakes—I made big ones. I divorced my daughter's father, for which I don't think she ever forgave me. I remarried a few years later, and once again I did not choose wisely, so again I divorced. Thankfully, my second husband and I can still see each other out in public and speak kindly to one another. In fact, when my daughter first left, he was one of my very first supporters, and he told me that he told her, "Your mother loves you more than anything on this earth. Call her and work this out." I truly appreciated that. I asked a known lesbian to move into my house with her children in the belief she loved me and would do anything in the world for me. I thought her children needed a strong influence of goodness, and I kidded myself into thinking I could be that influence. This so-called friend, however, was just another manipulator in my life who saw a broken person and used my vulnerability to her advantage. Now, I look back on all this, and the only thing I did right was divorce Aurora's father. Had I seen God then, as I did in 2015, my life could have turned out so differently. Yet in talking with ministers and my therapists, if I hadn't made those mistakes, would I have been ready to hear God when I did?

# December 22, 2015—Digging Deep

"She is a beautiful piece of broken pottery, put back together by her own hands. And a critical world judges her cracks while missing the beauty of how she made herself whole again." —J. M. Storms

Have you ever had people in your life who don't listen to the words you are saying? They decide in their own minds what they want to believe or assume, and that's the truth they hold on to. Well, my life has been full of them—daughter, parents, friends, and spouses.

I've learned over the past year that you can be honest with your words and actions, telling people how you are feeling and what your life holds to be true for you, but they can't see it. Nor do they hear what you are saying. Now, the old me would take to heart the words of others being thrust upon me recently, make them my truth, and doubt myself. But this new me, the one found in Christ, will not relent. I will not let my past define me.

I've also learned, when people think what's in their heads to be true, it's because they do not want to face their own junk and admit they played a part in the downfall of a relationship. It's impossible to reason with them.

I've also learned if you make one mistake in the past, it will be used against you continuously until the day you die. Some people are incapable of forgiveness and leaving the past in the past, and even if you change and are honest with your feelings, it's easier for them to throw your past in your face and see you for what they believe you are, rather than who you truly have become.

I've also learned if you remain true to yourself and keep plugging away and being honest with what God wants for your life, He will sustain you through all the storms. This is true for so many reasons, and again, I will not let my past define me.

I've learned when you point out the truth as you know it to others, and they don't like what you are saying, you are the enemy, and they will assume and attack anything of your character to prove their point. The old me would continue to argue and fight for my character, but not anymore. God sees the truth; He knows what's in my heart, and this is what allows me to continue to move forward and not look back.

I've also learned when you tell people they are "acting like others in your life," they don't want to be compared to those other people, yet they cannot change their actions toward you—and thus prove your point. They want to accuse, criticize, and verbally attack, and they do not hear what you are saying and what's in your heart to be told.

I've been accused, criticized, compared, and verbally dragged back into my old life, and no one is listening. I'm remaining strong. I'm holding fast to God's promise He will never leave, and He will sustain me.

I know it's hard to look at someone whom you love and think, "Wow, I may have hurt this person." To save face and not look at reality, you need to keep that person in a bad light. Believe me, I've done that. Now, I have big enough shoulders to bear any accusation that comes my way. I feel no need to fight off harsh words, slander, or what anyone feels is the "truth" because I know the truth in my heart, and God knows the truth.

Am I a little hurt? Yes. People say, "I know the real you," but if they did, and they heard and saw the transformation in my heart and life to this point, they would understand I've changed. Instead of running, like I would have in the past, I faced my fears, spoke my truth, and continued to move forward. My therapist tells me this is the best thing I could have ever done, and thank God for her, because she has heard the worst of my life, has seen me cry over mistakes I have made, and has never left my side or made me think I was selfish or unjust for facing issues that needed to be faced head-on. I powered through, released myself of blame for all that has gone wrong, and realized it does take three to make a relationship: God, you, and whomever else you choose to have in your life.

So go ahead and accuse. But remember that God calls us to "bear with each other and forgive whatever grievances you may have against one another. Forgive as the Lord forgave you. And over all these virtues, put on love, which binds them all together in perfect unity" (Colossians 3:13–14 NIV). I have chosen to forgive all those who keep accusing, blaming, and being unforgiving of me. I know who walked into my life and when they walked in, and I know who walked out of my life and exactly the moment I decided to let them go for my own sanity. It gets easier every day to let go of those who want to continue to accuse, persecute, and blame. Maybe it's because I know the truth in my heart and I know I've done my best. And yes, it does hurt to let go, but only because I know those who continue to cut me down have no idea of the grace I've experienced, the storm I have been through to get to this point in my life. I am eternally grateful for those who have heard my entire story and supported, loved, and extended forgiveness, grace, and helped me realize I am not the only person on the face of the planet who has made mistakes, fallen short, and learned to rest, reflect, and repent. This grace does not get extended by those who simply go to church on Sundays. It's extended by those who are true followers of Christ, not fans.

I have learned music is my saving grace. It takes me to places I need, takes me to places of peace and tranquility, and speaks to my heart when no one else is around. God always sends the song I need to hear at just the right time. As I was reflecting on yesterdays this morning, this song came on the radio. Again, I thank God for God and for sending what we need to hear at just the right time. The song "Soar" by Meredith Andrews is a beautiful song about God holding on to us, and when we put our trust in Him, we do soar high on the wings of eagles.

I need to continue to follow His path and listen to my heart, not the voices on my phone, the voices in my e-mail, the voices of my past, or the voices in my head at times. I'm fearfully and wonderfully made, and I have a new life to live. I was buried and raised, and God has me. I learned this on June 20, 2015, and I will continue to follow His path.

Even today, remembering whom I belong to is difficult. It isn't easy living with the knowledge my mistakes have completely broken my entire family apart. I'm to blame for all the strife, all the brokenness, my selfish ways, my thoughts, my path in life. As my parents age, I realize time is short. Will this family ever be put back together again? I carry guilt, shame, regret, and heartache. It takes a huge amount of effort for me to realize I may have put wheels in motion, but I'm not the only one who has a hand in the brokenness. Different words could have been spoken; situations could have been handled differently. Even today, words could be spoken, and hearts could be healed. But it's not completely up to me. Other people must have their hearts lined up with forgiveness and grace.

## *December 25, 2016—What Did Mary Know?*

"**M**ary, did you know?" What a song. Did Mary fully comprehend what God was telling her when He came to her and told her she would carry His Son? Did Mary fully comprehend all that Jesus would do when she was given the honor of carrying God's Son? What exactly was the full conversation between God and Mary? I know the Bible gives us glimpses, but I wonder sometimes if Mary said, "Seriously, God? You want me to carry a child who will die on a cross and suffer a horrible death to save the world?" And God said, "Yes," and Mary said, "Okay."

When you think of all Jesus did—walked on water, healed the sick, raised the dead, made the blind to see, calmed storms with just the wave of a hand, walked in heaven with the angels, and so much more—did Mary grasp this with all her might? Did she feel somewhat scared, happy, or overwhelmed?

I think about all this, and my heart beats just a little faster. I don't know if I could have listened to God tell me I would carry a child and then watch Him be persecuted, die on a cross, and rise again, just to save a sinner like me. I don't know if I could answer as Mary did: "I am the Lord's servant, may your word to me be fulfilled" (Luke 1:38 NIV).

Then, Mary, being nine months pregnant, has to go traveling on the donkey to Bethlehem to give birth to this perfect human in a manger full of straw, with animals around her and no midwife, no doctor, and no family. I can see myself now, telling Joseph, "Are you out of your mind? I am not riding a donkey through the cold and giving birth in a strange hotel!" I'm sure she was scared, but did the comfort of knowing God was with her make everything lighter? It certainly does lighten my burdens.

I think about the lyrics to "Breath of Heaven," where Mary asks if a wiser person should have taken her place, but Mary continues to believe, offers herself to God, and asks God to help her be strong in His plan. And what a plan He had!

I think about God's plan for my own life, and how I tried to live it on my own and do what I wanted to do instead of listening to the inner voice of God telling me to let go and let Him. I think about how I lived my way, and nothing seemed to go right. I think about how I gave my life to Him fully over the past year, and how much better life goes when I simply let go and let Him lead my path. I think about all the people, situations, and turmoil this past year has brought, and then I think about how peaceful I have become since He rules every aspect of my life. I see how people can't seem to grasp this peace I have found and how I do not feel the need to explain myself anymore. I don't feel the need to explain, argue, bicker, or justify myself because I know God has His plan, and my hope is found in Him.

I wonder if Mary felt the need to explain. Joseph could have had her stoned to death, but he didn't. I wonder if Mary felt the stares and heard people talk behind her back, call her names, and question her character, integrity, and heart. When I think about all this, my problems don't seem so big at all. I haven't been called to carry the Son of God; all I've been called to do is live the way the Bible tells me to, listen to God when He tells me to move, and love Him with all my heart ... and I do.

For some reason, this holiday season has found me focusing on Mary—what she experienced, what she was thinking, how she had so much stacked against her. Yet she remained strong. I think about how, as a mother, you must be strong for the sake of your children. I think about how God must have thanked her immensely for being such a noble woman and remaining true to Him. I think about my own life and what God has witnessed in my life. I realize all the times I thought I was experiencing something alone, I truly wasn't. God was walking with me every step of the way. He's had my back, my pain, and my joy. He was in the storm before it even began to rain in my life. I cannot begin to thank Him for enduring my pain and for giving me so much joy. I think about Him giving His only Son for our love, and it overwhelms my heart. I think of Mary and what she endured, and I can only look upon her with a humble admiration. She gave birth to the most precious gift I have ever been blessed with receiving. I cannot in good conscious take this gift lightly. Mother to mother, it's being given a heart transplant and receiving the gift of life, everlasting life, and all I need to do is give her Son my heart, my life, and my soul. That's a gift I will not return and will not take lightly. I hope as you think about the people involved in the first Christmas, you find someone you can identify with, someone you can relate, someone who touches your heart. This year for me, it's definitely Mary. My gift to her is to not dishonor her Son, to hold Him close to my heart, to love like He did, and to be thankful for the sacrifice His family made so I could take a breath.

# *January 6, 2016—Thank God for Redemption*

Okay, so I broke down on Sunday, December 27, 2015. I cried for about an hour, maybe longer. I remember hearing the 3:45 bell chime and the 4:00 bell chime, and I don't really remember anything else until the 5:00 bell chimed. Sunday resulted in many an anniversary date, and what more could I do but give in and let go? As I cried, I was filled with emotions such as shame, regret, failure, being unworthy, and sadness. I listened to the words of the one with me (my then fiancé), and I kept repeating what was being said: "God is here, I am here." I wondered, If God was really here, why was my heart hurting so bad? These feelings subsided, and I was able to fix dinner. I turned on a few of my favorite songs, "Held" by Natalie Grant followed by "Cry Out to Jesus" by Third Day. Then I broke down again and asked for an out loud prayer. Nothing like hearing someone pray out loud for you—and to not only hear the words but feel the words in your heart.

I went home, went to bed, and had a mostly prayerful night, listening to my heart and God's promises. It's funny how one event can bring a rush of emotions back. It's time to let go of them all, however, because I am redeemed. I am not who I once was, and I don't want to be who I once was. I don't want to live in shame, regret, and feelings of being unlovable and unworthy. Monday morning, I was met with a sermon about how the Bible is the only truth by Dave Stone, and several songs came on the radio that brought peace to my heart. I picked up my head and told the devil to get out of my head. He has no room in my head, my heart, and my home. He has no room in my life. He has no space to fill. He is not good; he is not worthy of my time. I will not allow—no, God will not allow anyone or anything to fill the space in my heart or head with negativity, shame, or regret. He will not let me be dragged into the past. I am not my past, I am not defined by my past, and I can have hope for a brighter future.

I've learned we bind ourselves by our pasts. God doesn't.

I've learned we let the devil in. God doesn't.

I've learned we don't allow in forgiveness. God does.

I've learned I am my own worst enemy. God isn't.

I'm looking forward to 2016. A whole new journey is waiting for me, and I'm ready to embrace it all.

I met a wonderful man. In my DC class, a lady came in one night and asked if anyone knew someone who would want to date a man who was almost fifty, owned his own home, had a wonderful job and a truck, and had never been married or had children. The entire class looked around and said, "Lucy." I agreed to meet this man, and a date was set up. He wound up being someone I had had a crush on in high school, so I went on the blind date. He was so handsome, and his name was strong, but I never believed he would want to go out with this wallflower! We began and ended each date in the parking lot at church. We prayed before each date, and he called at bedtime to pray again. By November 4, 2015, he asked me to marry him under the cross at our church. When we met, I liked him a lot. He was quiet, reserved, and very smart. We had a lot in common, yet we had very little in common. But we had a common thread: Jesus. He took all my past hurts and sorrow and placed them in his hands to carry with me. So yes, it was a whirlwind romance, but God was at the center of our relationship from the very beginning, and God has continued to be cornerstone.

## *January 8, 2016—Christmas Day and Love*

Christmas Day came and went without my daughter, Aurora. It's the second one without her, and it's something I never dreamed I would endure. As I was talking to a friend about my earthly family on Christmas Eve, I realize they do not see me as Christ does (and probably never will). They certainly don't love as Christ does, and that's not a healthy relationship to be in. I thought that if my salvation depends on whether or not I continue on a path to continue to let them verbally berate me, then the answer is no. I do forgive all their trespasses, and I have a pure heart when it comes to how I love them because I see them as Christ does: forgiven, imperfect, and flawless. I can extend grace.

I miss Aurora. I miss her smile, I miss her laugh, and I miss her perspective on life. I wonder, if she could and would see me now, what her thoughts would be on all I've been through since my divorce to her father in 2004. I know this new life I have found in Christ is where she wanted me to be and recognizing myself through His eyes is what she wanted me to see, how through life in Him we can be loved. I believe in my heart she would be so incredibly happy and proud because her mom finally gets it.

I think about all the bad relationships I have been in with those who cannot love as Christ does, and how this past year was a true transformation for me. I want to encourage all of you out there who are struggling with relationships where you are not loved as Christ loves: Get out. Do not continue the path I was for so long. My normal was if people weren't being mean or telling me how wrong I am about life, not fully respecting me or my beliefs, then they weren't fully loving me. Now, I realize how unhealthy a path that was, and although it's difficult at times to realize I deserve to be loved, it's a true honor to be in healthy, loving, compassionate, grace-filled relationships, and I am learning to accept them. It's not easy to let the good, positive love in, but I will eventually learn that I am worth every ounce that is pouring in.

I heard a Christmas song the other night, and it's been a long time since I've heard it, but the words simply state that God is "in us, for us and with us ... His name is Immanuel."

God is in us. Yes, He is. He is in our hearts, all we need to do is embrace it.

God is for us. Yes, God is for us in every situation. He doesn't leave us, even when we stray. He doesn't keep records of our wrong, and when we turn to Him, He wraps His arms around us and holds on tight.

God is with us. Immanuel. God is with us. Immanuel. Every step we take, every situation we endure, every harsh word spoken, every tear we cry, and every joy we experience, God is with us.

As I reflected on all I was blessed with from the start of the day to very end, I realized how loved I really am, and how many people out there I genuinely love. After this past year of resting, repenting, and reflecting, I know how blessed I am. I was given a gift years ago of forgiveness, salvation, and genuine, pure love when God sent His Son to save the world. God was literally with us then, and He is certainly with us now. It doesn't matter if it's Christmas Day, Easter, or any other religious holiday we choose to celebrate; God is with us daily, hourly, and moment to moment.

A friend said to me the other day, "You are very important to a lot of people." I never realized I was important, I mattered, and my heart meant something to people. Now I see it. Now I get it. Now I want all that love, and I want to matter. I'm finding my way home.

My heart feels at peace, my steps are lighter, and my mornings are brighter. I wake up, pray, and thank God for all He has given me for the day—before the day even begins.

It used to be that when I was in a relationship, I still felt lonely. The loneliness never really went away. Now, even when I am by myself, I am not lonely. I know someone is with me every moment of every day. It could be a friend, a coworker, or a brother or sister in Christ, but for the first time, I know that when no one else is around, God surrounds me with His arms, His love, and His grace.

Michael W. Smith has a song titled "When Love Takes You In," and it so true. You can search your entire life and seek for a home to call your own. You can cry yourself to sleep, drift off, and dream. But when love takes you in, everything truly changes. A miracle truly starts with the beat of a heart that knows and, more important, feels it belongs. My heart is so full right now. I feel like crying happy tears and continuously thanking those around me for believing in me, accepting me, and pushing me to become all I should become, all I could become. There is nothing like fully coming into your own and realizing your potential in what God has made you to become. And then to know those around you are loving you as God made you … well, this is the type of love that never lets go, Frankly, I don't plan on letting it go.

I encourage everyone to let love take you in, let God wrap His arms around your heart and your entire being. Let God show you who you are and what you are, and you'll learn how to love yourself. When you love yourself, it's so easy to let others love you too.

I'll leave you with this: Find love, people.

Finding love and truly accepting love came slowly for me. To realize I was worth love took a while to learn for some reason. I don't know at what moment in my life I concluded I wasn't loved and accepted, but for some reason, this was my delusional thinking. Whether it's the child abuse, being fat and ugly in school, not being a person with lots of friends or a thousand social media followers, I don't know. But there were people whom I've known for twenty-plus years who stuck with me no matter what, and I still have these people today. I'm glad they saw my potential and decided to stay by me.

## February 5, 2016—Not Broken with C. S. Lewis

What a beautiful quote I read tonight as I was doing my DC homework. It's funny: I've had trouble writing lately because I've had too many thoughts wrapping around my brain, mainly because I'm fighting Satan at every angle of my life. I do not want to go back to my old life, and one tiny slip will sent me spiraling out of control into the dark again. I've had trouble writing because I keep thinking about a text I received from what I thought was one of my best friends and someone I loved dearly, although she recently told me I did not love her (I guess because I chose a different path than what even I expected). Her text read, "You are right, I do not know you. The person I know is gone. Very sad."

Really? You prefer the broken me over the newly healed me? You prefer the person who would let everyone walk all over her and not give her any respect? You prefer the person who was sad all the time? You prefer the person who tried to be perfect at all the time yet received no thanks, no praise, no recognition? You prefer the person who was spiraling down to a depression no one could save her from?

This same "friend" then went on to tell me how I had lied to her and to my therapist, yet she doesn't want to be put into the same category as others from my past who also do not see the new me, the free me, the saved me.

I've shown several people who know my story the text about the old me being gone, and they all say the same thing: "Hallelujah!" Yes, my therapist may have just been, as someone recently pointed out sarcastically, a licensed clinical social worker, but she helped saved me. Weekly visits followed by biweekly visits, finally ending in "Hey, Lucy, you've got this. You are where you are supposed to be. You can keep coming here, but I really have nothing else to offer." What, I'm cured? Why, how can you say that? She could say that because I did the work, I did the homework, and I did the resting, reflecting, and repenting. Not only was I seeing her, but I was meeting twice a week with my Christian family, who drove me toward God's word so I could see that I was worth something to my Lord and Savior. He sees me. He knows my worth, and more important, He knows my name!

I also recently saw a Facebook post that read, "'Never run back to what broke you.' —Toby Mac."

Never run back to what broke you. Hmm … To me, that explains a lot. I've spent forty-six, almost forty-seven years running back to what broke me. I have tried to live up to everyone's expectations and have not given too much thought as to what God thought of me, or what I even think of me. Last March, it hit so hard, and in April it hit even harder. In May, when I decided to give my life to Christ, it wasn't a whim or a "Oh, hey, let's try this for a while." It was, "I'm all in on this and need to do better. I need to really focus on the one man who gave His one and only Son for my undying, undivided, 100 percent attentive love!"

I've been accused of lying, cheating, not fully disclosing who I am to people, and having mental instability, bipolar disorder, or multiple personality disorder. I've heard people say to my therapist, "Do you know what we've been through with this one?" Really? Do these same people know what God has gone through waiting for us, and what we have done to disrespect God? To run from Him and try to live on our own? To try to prove to God that "I've got this; I don't need you"? It's okay. Go ahead and view me as you want. I know the truth, God certainly knows the truth, and if you opened your eyes, listened, saw, heard, and watched me, you'd see too.

So, yes, in the past I have accepted excuses for what I have done too easily. I've been too hard on others and not accepted their excuses for what I believed has wronged me, and I have forgiven because Christ forgave me. But that does not mean I'll go running back to what broke me. No way, no how. I finally see me for what God sees, and that's a very valuable, lovable, grace-filled creation. I am worthy, and I will not be broken—not again. God is with me, and I plan to remain in Him forever.

## *February 12, 2016—I'll Stand Here*

"I stand here at your feet I'm laying down the fear in me and as your child claiming peace oh give this heart your victory I stand here, I stand here." — Lauren Daigle, "I Stand Here"

It's funny. I was just speaking to my husband last night about fear and love. I told him I truly realize for the first time in my life, I'm not afraid of someone. He knows all my junk and doesn't hold it against me or bring it up in conversation. I'm the only one who does that, and that's when I let Satan have control of my thoughts. I'm learning how to stop those thoughts, though. First it's with prayer, and then it's by telling myself, "I'm standing before God, and He sees my heart and my life. I fear no evil." I repeat this process about one hundred times a day, if not more.

I realized this after reading 1 John, specifically verse 4:18 (NIV), "There is no fear in love, but perfect love drives out fear, because fear has to do with punishment. The one who fears is not made perfect in love."

Wow. I grew up in fear and thinking if I did one thing wrong, love would be taken away. This fear carried into my marriages, friendships, and sometimes other personal relationships, and everyone has proven this to be true. Love was used to gain something from me. People knew if I felt the threat of the love going away, I would be under their control. If I am fearing, however, that is not love.

Now I know the difference between real, perfect love and imperfect love. Now I understand why I spent years searching for love and acceptance for no reason, and a lot of time in the wrong places with the wrong people. Last year, I had an epiphany of sorts. I gained knowledge and took a deep look at my life and what was wrong with it and what I was striving for. Not only was I hurting myself, but I was hurting others in the process. I had people tell me to be completely honest with them at all times, and I finally found the honesty. I thought I was living fearfully, but I soon learned that being honest and stating how you see the world, how you see your life, and how you see their life was not going to work with those who weren't living in and with Christ. Now I truly understand that love, and I started to embrace it last April, when I was baptized. I made a promise to myself to never go back to what broke me, and I'm not. I see God's love, I feel God's love, and all I can continue to say is, How great is His love? How great is my relationship with Him? How great is knowing I am made new and perfect, and He sees me as flawless?

It is funny to me that I knew my husband was the one for me in less than two weeks after meeting him. I know he felt the same because not only was he walking with God, but he was searching for a woman growing and seeking God's heart. It wasn't that we fell in love, as people say. I've learned through my marriage class at my church that people who fall in love will also fall out of love, and this too has proven to be true. If you can't share your love and knowledge of God in relationships, they will not work, no matter how hard you try. It's broken from the start, and it can be healed only through God's grace and mercy.

So yes, this love thing is new for me … the perfect, fearless love. I don't fear anyone or anything anymore, and when I do, my husband reminds me the evil one will try to steal our joy and make us feel less than that perfect love. I stand here before God every morning and know I have to lay down the fear because if I don't, I'm not letting love win. I have come to realize people use threats, chaos, past mistakes you have made, and their own assumptions to cast fear in your path and bring you back to the person you once were before you found your life in Christ. I have found people don't see the transformation you have made, the caterpillar becoming the butterfly. They hold you captive in their cocoon of anger, hurt, and they feel justified in what they are doing because they refuse to see. Last night, after our night of worship at church, I had several of my husband's friends tell me to stay strong and not let anyone rob my joy. God has it all, and I can rest in their prayers and God's promises. I also realize now I need to pray for these people who try to attack because they are not experiencing perfect, fearless love. I have a cloud of witnesses surrounding me and bringing peace and fearless love.

I will continue to claim peace as God's child, and I will continue to stand before God and let all fear go. I am not broken; He breathes His life into me. I am continuing to exclaim, "Your kingdom come." I am His child. He surrounds me, He protects me, and He gave me victory.

# April 7, 2016—The Communication of Hearts

Recently I found out a member of my earthly family had a medical issue. My heart encouraged me to send a small note of encouragement. Granted, this person had sent me a text on Christmas morning 2014 and told me to never contact her again, but I wanted her to know if she died, I at least cared and would pray.

That's who I am: I love you even when you show me hate.

And speaking of communication, why is it so hard for people to ask you what's in your heart, what's on your mind? I went through a period of time where I didn't talk too much, I kept a lot of things bottled up inside, and then I started talking (in therapy) about life, decisions, experiences, and expectations. Now, at times you can't shut me up. When I joined the table group I now colead last January, I talked even more because these people were Christian, listened, gave advice, and led me to scripture that helped heal.

I find it funny that people I am acquainted with call others to find out what I'm doing, how I'm feeling, or what's going on in my life. Did I suddenly start speaking a foreign language when we talk? I also love how you tell others something about you, and they have to "check up" on you to verify the information. Really? Why ask me about my life, then? Go find your own "expert" on my life. But remember, you shut down communication, not me.

And speaking of communication, how many does it take to communicate? I always believed two. I talk, you listen; you talk, I listen. Funny how it works that way, huh? I find if I don't understand something, I ask or repeat back to you. Is this old-fashioned or outdated?

I also have a hard time when communication is handled like this: "You tell me about your life. I will verify with my sources to make sure what you feel about your life and what's going on in your life is correct." I recently had a "friend" who called and stated, "Since you rich new husband paid off your car, where is your money for this, that, or something else?" Well, in actuality my car isn't paid off; it's refinanced, and would you like a copy of those papers? No, you don't want a copy of the papers? You don't want to speak to my husband? Why not? Afraid to hear the truth? Well, then, don't accuse me of something you know nothing about.

I also recently had a friend who told me I need to let people treat me however they want and talk to me however they want because that is simply how life is. Did you also call them and tell them to accept me for me and see how my life has changed? No? Then don't ask me to do something you haven't asked them to do.

All this leads me to thinking about past decisions I have made and what I regret. I don't know whether regret is really the right word; there are certainly decisions I would change that could change the course of my current situation. For example, I wouldn't have married the second time. There were certainly red flags everywhere, but I ignored them in search of something I didn't quite understand myself. I would move to the town my daughter graduated from high school, but I wouldn't have bought a house; renting would be good enough. I would still get my two dogs, and my daughter's cat, but that would be it. I definitely would not have asked anyone to move in with us to help share expenses and life—that decision could change how my life is now.

There are so many issues, decisions, and regrets my heart has healed from, and it would be wonderful to tell my story to my others and have them hear how God has completely changed my life. If I could communicate with some, I would share how my daughter walking out of my life changed my heart and opened my eyes to even more things I wasn't seeing clearly. I would share how the church's current Bible study series showed me I was worth God's love, mercy, and grace—something I had never felt or understood before. But you can't communicate with people who want to keep you in the past and who don't want to hear how your life and heart have changed, what God did for you, and how you plan to move forward with your life. You just can't.

To me, it's funny how these same people want to tell you how people in their own lives or churches have been changed through the power of prayer or God, but they don't want to hear about your story. What's with that? I would think the people you'd be most happy about having a significant life change and aha God moments are your family!

You also cannot communicate with people who want only to determine what your life is about by talking to other people about your life. Whenever I want to know something, I go straight to that person and say, "Hey, how's it going? What's going on with you?" Doesn't seem that hard, does it?

A really good friend's best friend died, and I sent a note saying, "I heard about your friend. Sorry for you loss. Hope you can keep his memory alive by making the crosses and boxes." A family member was having a heart procedure soon, and I sent her a note stating, "I was very sorry to hear about your recent health issues. I'm sure it's been a little scary. My husband, in-laws, and I will be praying for you and your recovery. From what I understand it should only be about a week to ten days before you're up and running again! Good luck! Thoughts and prayers!"

That was almost two weeks ago, and still no reply from that either. Yet people still want to tell me how I should handle everyone and that I should keep doing more and keep putting myself out there to be rejected and stomped on. I'm thinking God doesn't want me to continue to be beat down; at least, that's what the New International

Version of the Bible I read says. I come back to my all-time favorite verses, Romans 5:1–11.

---

Therefore, since we have been justified through faith, we [a] have peace with God through our Lord Jesus Christ, through whom we have gained access by faith into this grace in which we now stand. And we [b] boast in the hope of the glory of God. Not only so, but we [c] also glory in our sufferings, because we know that suffering produces perseverance; perseverance, character; and character, hope. And hope does not put us to shame, because God's love has been poured out into our hearts through the Holy Spirit, who has been given to us.

You see, at just the right time, when we were still powerless, Christ died for the ungodly. Very rarely will anyone die for a righteous person, though for a good person someone might possibly dare to die. But God demonstrates his own love for us in this: While we were still sinners, Christ died for us.

Since we have now been justified by his blood, how much more shall we be saved from God's wrath through him! For if, while we were God's enemies, we were reconciled to him through the death of his Son, how much more, having been reconciled, shall we be saved through his life! Not only is this so, but we also boast in God through our Lord Jesus Christ, through whom we have now received reconciliation.

---

My heart has taken a few twists and turns over the past year, and all for the good, all for the better. In so many ways, it has healed, but it's still cracked from not having my child in my life, and I am discovering it is a wound that will never heal. I'm glad my parents can be without me and not reach out, not send a note or card, or make a phone call, and their hearts are fine. I have a hard time believing those people who say they miss me because their actions definitely say something else. I'm glad my sister cannot talk to me and her heart is great! I'm glad certain "friends" can find peace in talking to ex-friends and neighbors about my life and gossiping about me, and they find comfort in their "truth."

In the healing of hearts, I find myself amazed at people who tell me I'm doing great, I've come a long way, and I have held my own during the darkest time of my life. And when asked what I wish my former friends would do, I find myself coming back again and again to the story of the prodigal son. Specifically, I was recently asked what I will say to Aurora if she ever calls. My answer was simple: the same thing I wish my parents would have said to me, the same thing the father of the prodigal son said to him, and the same thing I know my Father in heaven says to me on a daily basis.

> But while he was still a long way off, his father saw him and was filled with compassion for him; he ran to his son, threw his arms around him and kissed him.
>
> The son said to him, "Father, I have sinned against heaven and against you. I am no longer worthy to be called your son."
>
> But the father said to his servants, "Quick! Bring the best robe and put it on him. Put a ring on his finger and sandals on his feet. Bring the fattened calf and kill it. Let's have a feast and celebrate. For this son of mine was dead and is alive again; he was lost and is found." So, they began to celebrate. (Luke 15:20–22 NIV)

This father didn't say, "Let me tell you every way you hurt me." He didn't say, "Do you know what you put me through?" He didn't say,

"Do you know how wrong you were?" He opened his arms, hugged his child, and said, "Welcome home."

It's funny how God closes doors of communication but opens ones of full honesty, disclosure, and acceptance. And it's amazing how this heals your life. I'm living proof. That seems to be my theme song, "I'm living proof," and I am. I am proof a person can be so broken, and God heals. I'm living proof that you can be scared and shamed by things in your life, and God heals. I'm living proof that when you surround yourself with people who truly walk with Christ, you are enveloped in mercy and grace.

Yes, I am living proof of abuse, shame, bad decisions (and a lot of good ones too), trying hard to live as Christ would want me too, and never quite getting it right. I'm so glad Christ came to walk among the sick, the wounded, and the sinful. If he only came to walk with the just, healthy, and righteous, where would any of us be?

I do daily checks on my heart. Is there anything I need to evaluate, anyone I need to talk to? I think about how I communicate, and I wonder whether I have left any stone unturned. Does my daughter know how I feel? Have I made myself clear to her that I love her and expect nothing from her? How many unanswered e-mails do I have to send before I give up? Have I fully rested, reflected, repented, and done my best to reconcile? Do I feel the need to constantly put myself in the path of those who don't love as Christ loves and to be berated and belittled, to be the only one who takes responsibility for actions? Is the weight of the entire world and every mistake ever made in every relationship my fault?

Those are heavy questions, and, for the longest time, I would answer yes to all of them. Now that I know Christ and what He asks us each to do, I can say the following.

- Yes, there are people I need to speak to (Aurora, Luke).

- No, I haven't left any stone unturned. I will keep turning stones until Aurora is back.

- Yes, Aurora should have a clear picture of the fact that I just want a relationship with her, I expect nothing, and I am sorry for whatever I have done to cause her heart to hate.

- Yes, I'll send a gazillion e-mails before I give up.

- Yes, I have done the four Rs.

- No, I do not feel the need to put myself in the path of anyone who feels the need to berate, belittle, and not take responsibility for their actions.

- No, the weight of the world and every mistake ever made is certainly not my fault.

It took a long time to realize these things and to come with terms with the fact that I am loved so dearly and deeply by God. It took a shorter amount of time to realize when you surround yourself with those who walk with Christ, you'll be able to accept the love and grace showered upon you. God gave me a great gift when my heart opened, I heard the truth spoken, and I saw the love coming down.

I'll leave you with these thoughts.

Check your heart—how's it beating? Is there someone you need to call? Someone you need to write? Someone you need to talk to because you've only listened to gossip? Someone you've gossiped about whom you may need to apologize to? Someone you may have spoken harshly to, and maybe you should ask forgiveness? Hebrews 8:12 says, "For I will forgive their wickedness and I will remember their sins no more."

Do a heart check. Forgive, and make that call. It may change the life of someone else, but better yet, it may change yours.

In the days since my daughter has come back, my parents and I have had some pretty good conversations about the mistakes we all have made, and we have tried to put our new selves back together again. We have all grown and admitted our regrets, but we will not love or live in regret. We need to move forward and see one another for who we are, not what we remember of one another. It feels good to hear my parents say they are sorry for their part in our broken relationship. We all promise to handle future miscommunications differently and to be open and honest at all times.

## *July 12, 2016—Two-Way Street to a Wedding*

Have you ever seen the sign for a one-way street? Ever wondered what it would be like if you took only one-way streets and never two-way streets? I have learned over the past eighteen months a lot of people only travel one-way streets. Some people travel two-way streets, and thank God for this because my daughter called! Yes, folks, that's right: my daughter has returned, and I keep driving to her, and her to me. A two-way street!

It's been a whirlwind of activity, stress, love, stress, new beginnings, stress, and learning who my daughter is again. She's really great, and I have learned not all told to me was exactly accurate, but that's okay. Like I told her, communicating through others is not a relationship. Only face-to-face and phone connections will heal us, and it is healing and growing, and it's wonderful. It's a two-way street!

Her wedding plan at the church she was attending fell through, so my husband and I scrambled to find a venue, food, and photographer, and it was truly a beautiful event. The kids asked my husband to perform the ceremony, and though hesitant at first, he accepted and truly made the day special and memorable. I read what he wrote often, not only to remind Aurora during difficult marital situations but to remind myself of what a wonderful, Christian, loving man I have in my life.

But I digress and get off the subject of streets. There is so much to convey, relay, and rejoice about right now, and I have no clue where to begin, but I feel the one-way or two-way street is a beginning. It brought joy to my heart to hear Aurora had been following my blog, so she knew how I was feeling for some time. It would have been nice, I've told her, if she would have clued me in at all so I could know what was on her mind, but we have the rest of my life to explore her thoughts and feelings. I have been told people read my blog and ask Aurora to interpret my feelings. That's a one-way street. Call *me* if you want to know how I feel; my child cannot answer for me, just as I cannot answer for her. But like I said, some cars only travel one-way streets.

I have been informed the book I gave my parents to read at our counseling session, which completely changed my life, was given to someone at their church to read and interpret for them. So much for my parents asking me why the book changed my life, how it changed my life, what I learned from reading it, and how it grew me, saved me, and comforted me. The man who read it doesn't even know me, nor has he called to ask how, what, why, or when about the book. Again, this is a perfect example of a one-way street.

In the weeks leading to the wedding, we had many small side streets to travel, traffic lights that were only red, and highways leading to nowhere—venue, food, photographers, and several people dropped out of the wedding for their "Christian" values and morals. My husband and I kept telling the kids, "Where is grace?" and explaining to them what we meant by grace. Aurora had some relatives who were supposed to participate in the wedding, but due to my attendance and participation, they dropped out of their duties or threatened to not come. My response was the same over and over again. "Aurora, I do not have to attend your wedding if it is easier and less stressful to you and Luke." Her response was the same every time: "Mom, I want you there. If other people don't want to come because of you, that's their problem." We not only hosted a wedding, but we rejoiced in the union of Aurora and Luke. What gets me the most is the comment someone made to Aurora in the days before the wedding that went something to the effect of, "Your mom abandoned you and the entire family. It'll be awkward to be with her." Seriously? Thank you, Aurora, for setting that statement straight. I'm glad she had the guts to inform this person that she'd left me and that I was specifically told not to contact anyone in that particular person's family.

Yes, I was completely overwhelmed during the week of the wedding, but my husband and I prayed every morning and every night. I had my family in Christ praying for us, the kids, and the entire situation, and because of these prayers, I knew the day would be what the kids wanted it to be.

The day before the wedding, we didn't have the bride, we had the groom, and it was completely awesome. The morning of the wedding, my husband fixed him breakfast. We gave him a card and were able to pray with him. As we were driving to the venue, I wondered how my daughter was feeling and whether she was nervous. We texted a bit, and when I arrived at the venue and found her, she was snippy, grumpy, and jittery. She looked at me and said, "Blah, blah, blah—just hug me," so I did.

My husband and I prayed the morning of the wedding the day would be exactly what the kids wanted it to be, and I feel they did receive the wedding they wanted because at 9:15 p.m. on their wedding night, they called from their hotel just to say thanks for their day. Of course, that made me cry because you want your daughter to have a beautiful wedding, and I believe she did! As for gaining a son, I believe we gave him the best day possible too.

At her wedding, of course I had to approach people first. Of course no one would take a step toward me. Some family members only gave me a glare (there's the old one-way street again). And really, it's fine. These people didn't communicate one bit when Aurora was gone, so why worry with them now? The only people I cared about seeing were my parents. I said my hellos, introduced my husband, and that was that. I requested my table be set aside from others (mainly for their comfort, not mine), and Aurora agreed. We picked out my "family table" the night of rehearsal. I was surrounded by those who have walked with me through the darkest of times and rejoiced with me during my happy times, and it was such a joy to celebrate my daughter's return and wedding with them—a beginning of new life for all of us. These people haven't left my side through the good, the bad, and the ugly. They do not judge, condemn, ignore, give books to others to read, question my motives or my sanity, or sit around and analyze me. They love, extend grace, show Christian love, and help grow me. It is a beautiful, two-way street.

In the weeks since the wedding, the kids have been unfriended on Facebook (is this really a big deal? I think not, but it still hurts at times and fuels their anger), been given ultimatums, been ignored, been judged, and shared their experiences over the past eighteen months. It's been stressful, relieving, insightful, sad, and hurtful for them, and it's hard to see them struggle with my past mistakes, their mistakes, being condemned for talking to and forming a new relationship with me, and being completely ignored by some. It's good to know people sat around and discussed my mental state, my thoughts, my feelings, and my mistakes; people judged me, condemned me, discussed what type of counseling I needed, and came to conclusions about my life, my life experiences, and how those experiences shaped me without asking me to participate. (You see the one-way street here?)

Am I surprised at any of this? Nope.

Am I shocked? Not really.

Am I hurt? Of course.

Does it really matter? Not in the way you would think.

The past eighteen months have shown me who really cares and who will be there when the lights on the street turn dark. I've told the kids, Don't just keep those around who ride with you when you are happy and driving the freeway full of joy and no cares. Remember the ones who traveled with you in the dark, dank, scary streets—those are the people who will cross every bridge with you.

Life isn't perfect. I still have a bit of fear I will offend one of the kids, and they will never be heard from again. But I have an understanding with myself, and it was given to me by God. God didn't promise life would be perfect. He promised to walk with me through the storms. He promises to hold my hand and help guide my thoughts, words, and actions if I fully rely on Him. My husband tells me God has me first, He has me second, and He has the kids third, so with that, and prayer, where can I go wrong?

I put my trust in those thoughts totally. I may offend the kids (unintentionally, of course). I may make another mistake. But if I do, and they come to me and let me know, I can fix it, apologize, or both. Being in Christ isn't a Sunday thing, a "volunteer here and there" thing, a "pick up my Bible and give it a glance or two" thing. It's a daily thing, and knowing He has me, and I have Him … well, that's a two-way street with no exit ramp!

## September 4, 2016—Thy Will

I stay confused at times. I hear God speaking, and I know what I am supposed to do. I pray, go to church, stay in His word, and build my relationship with Him. So I wonder why, at times in my life, I have ended up not knowing how I ended up where I was mentally and spiritually. But then I remember Your heart hurts when I hurt. Sometimes four words is truly all we need to say, to thank you for hearing what we cannot speak: "Thy will be done." When I hurt, when I am at a loss for words, when nothing comforts, when I lost a child, when my child was diagnosed with disease, when I divorced, when my daughter ran away, when my family slammed doors … I have to remember that God is all powerful, all knowing, and all understanding. You give, You take away, You know what's best for us, and when it is best, and we should rejoice in pain and in sorrow when I am in the deepest despair. God does not promise life will be easy; He promises He will be with us in the storms.

Sometimes I have stop and remember that He is God and I am not. We have to remember that God sees us and hears us, and that His plans are good, and that He has only goodness in store for us.

The song "Thy Will" by Hillary Scott became a mantra for me. It is a very powerful song that we have to sing and repeat the words over to ourselves as we walk through storms. As I see those around me struggling, hurting, and trying to find God in the midst of pain, it's an acknowledgment to our Lord that no matter what we want for us, His will is always better, always best. His will is the only will we need to think about.

This song makes me think about my soft-hearted, kind, loving son-in-law and the wounds he has felt from a very young age—wounds from his parents, his friends, and his siblings (I see your pain, I understand your pain, I will walk you through this storm my son). I pray God will give him the answers he needs and that his heart longs to hear, and I know God's will and God's time is the best. My prayers are heard. God's will be done.

I think about my beautiful daughter and the wounds in her heart. There are wounds I have caused, which I acknowledge and have apologized for. I think about the restoration and acknowledgment she wants and needs in her life, for her heart to be softened. I pray knowing what she wishes, but I know that God's will and timing is best. I know she sees and feels my apologies and my validation of her feelings at all times. I know my prayers are heard. God's will be done.

I think about my friends who have struggled for years with infertility, who lost a pregnancy and now are awaiting their first children. I think about their strength and their acknowledgment that God's will is what they long for, and they will raise their children knowing who gave them these precious gifts. God heard their prayers. His will be done.

I think about my beautiful friend and the singer in David and my wedding, who is currently at the hospital with her very ill husband. My wishes, as I am sure all our wishes, are for him to recover, wake up, and say, "Thanks, Becca, for taking care of me." Then he will go back to sleep, and we will know God is healing him. Of course, deep down, I know God is healing him, but will that healing be so he is on this earth for another thirty years, or will God call him home to live with Him? I know my prayers are heard.

I think about my own wishes for my own life. I think about my marriage, my children, my future grandchildren, my friends, and my beautiful family in Christ. I know my wishes are heard, but it is certainly God's will that will prevail overall.

I think about the wounds of my own life and how He has restored them in His way—not the way I originally wished for them to be. But His will was done, and His will was much better than anything I could have wished or prayed. His answer to some relationships is for me to remain silent and continue to watch the actions and words of those who believe they have never done wrong, those who stand in judgment of me, my child, and my husband. I will remain in His will, staying silent.

I think about the future and what His will is. I know what doors He has closed, and He told me to rest easy because He will take care of opening those doors in His time. I can rest and know I've done my part.

I think about my sisters in Christ Jesus, why He brought them to my life, and how His will has empowered me with friends, family, and relationships in His name.

I find myself on my knees, wondering what His will is, praying for healing and restoration. I find myself at a loss for words in times of sadness and sorrow, and I know all I need to know and say is, "Your will be done, Lord," and my prayer is answered.

I hope when others look into my life, hear my story, and learn what areas of my life I asked for God for His will to be done, I hope it helps. I hope they see the mistakes, the faith, the waiting, and the hope, and that they know God's will is for us to be happy. He has not left us when we make a mistake, when we are wounded; He carries us and feels our pain. I understand now my mistakes, my hurt, my wounds, and my sorrow were a way to bring me closer to God, to be vulnerable and give Him my life—not my parents, not my exes, not my child, but God. He had my life from the very moment He knit me together. Now I understand His promises. I understand I have to stop and remember He is God. I need to remember He is in control.

I need to remember His will will always be done, and the sooner we succumb, the sooner we give ourselves to Him, the sooner we will experience a joy and goodness only He has in store for us. God's way is always, always better. He will give you what you need at just the right time. I can definitely attest to this goodness.

Are you ready to give your life to Him?

Are you ready for His will to be done in your heart?

Are you like a child on your knees?

Are you ready for the joy and goodness He has for your life?

Do you understand His plans are always for you?

No matter what your life is like right now, no matter your walk with others or with Christ, and no matter the mistakes, the hurt, the sorrow, and the joys, I encourage you to get on your knees and say four words: "Thy will be done." Repeat these words in the morning, noon and at night, and share your story of faith and hope. His will be done …

As of this posting, my friend's husband passed away. One more son has gone to sleep, to rest in the Father's arms, until we all meet in heaven to rejoice.

## October 30, 2016—Mission Trip to the Dominican Republic

Today was day one of being a warrior for God in the Dominican Republic. We traveled to a school and played with the kids. What was great was hearing and seeing the kids yell, "Hola, hola." The teachers didn't seem thrilled we were there, but the kids were amazing! One girl saw the cross tattoo on my arm, and the drawing began. I must have drawn sixty of them in all shapes, sizes, and colors. We ate lunch at camp, practiced our skit, and headed to the church for our princess camp. When we pulled up to the church, there was an older gentleman standing in his doorway, and he waved and shouted, "Hola, dios te ama!" (Hello, God loves you!), I waved and said it back to him. We had thirty-two girls, and some of their moms stayed. We played games, had a historic biblical story, and started our boxes. What I noticed most is that the moms seemed just as thrilled as the kids. The moms wanted to play the games and listened intently to our skit and lesson.

The language barrier is slightly annoying. With the kids you can't tell whether or not they speak English. But a sweet girl named Natalie speaks English well and wants to be a doctor. It's pretty awesome so far, especially having her interpret and teach Spanish to me.

Day two was rough. We visited a hospital, and the conditions are sad. When you go to the hospital, you take your own linens, towels, toilet paper, and (if you need it) blood. There is no air-conditioning and no ceiling fans. We visited with several families, and I was blessed to pray for a young man with dengue virus, a whole room full of ill men, and their families. Each man was happy we were there to pray. One of our leaders was praying for a man whose wife was in surgery, and he in turn started praying for us! What's awesome about the Dominicans is that they truly have hearts for Jesus—more heart than what I've personally witnessed in America.

On day three, I was sad that it seems the women here are so repressed. We saw a fourteen-year-old girl who was married with two kids. The women seem to have one job in most of the villages: raising their kids and sweeping. I wonder how many of these young girls had dreams of something more? Or are they completely happy with this life? Would I be happy raising kids and grandkids? If that was all I knew, would I wish for something more? I'm not 100 percent sure. Everyone here seems so happy, and people care for each other like a *Leave It to Beaver* society. I adore it. I definitely want to expand my Spanish so I can have a better, unbroken conversation!

On day four, we visited the children's hospital. Although there is no air-conditioning, there are ceiling fans. There are six to eight beds in every room. Again, it's the same: you bring your own linens, towels, and blood. There are no hospital gowns in either hospital.

I got to pray with Ganiel, who had a broken leg surgery today. He had a car accident and broke his leg below the knee. His mother and father were with him.

I met a young girl named Elliana with a broken leg due to boy at school pushing her down.

Then I met a man whose son, Mike, was in a car accident with his baby. His baby died, and Mike was critical.

I met another young girl in a car accident, and she'd hurt her leg, shoulder, and arm.

Yosayiti is seven with leukemia, and she needs bone marrow transplant. She had been three months since she'd found out she needed the transplant to come to America, but she has to apply for a visa and then figure out whether she will go to Miami or Boston. Her parents bought her blood, but it went bad, so they bought more. She got a transplant from her sister.

While I was observing and listening to other stories, there was a lady looking in our room and holding a young girl, maybe nine months old. She motioned for me to come over. I asked if she meant me, just to be sure, and she vehemently nodded. I walked over, and she started speaking, I said, "Lo siento, no habla español." ("Sorry, I do not speak Spanish"). She waved her hands, shook her head, and put her hands together in prayer and bowed her head. I put my hands together and said, "You want me to pray?"

"Si, si," ("Yes, yes") she said. I took her hand, put my hand on her child, and prayed. Afterward, I gave her some color sheets and crayons and asked if I could look at her daughter's x-ray to see if I could "entender." (understand). She said, "Si," so I looked. I saw that her daughter had a blockage not her intestines. I told her I would pray from America. She squeezed my hand. I turned and let the tears roll. There is no language barrier when you go to Dios in love and prayer.

I keep wondering what I learned from this trip. First and foremost, I didn't come thinking I would be a blessing; I came knowing I'd be blessed. The girls in our princess camp were awesome, but the moms even more so. While doing the skits and lessons and watching the moms and grandmas, I wondered whether anyone ever told them of their worth. I saw the looks on their faces and the tears in their eyes. They certainly know Jesus and His love for them. But do their husbands treat them like Christ does? From what I observed, no.

The girls in the hospital with babies … they were no older than eighteen, and some were as young as fourteen. Their lives are now raising children, cooking, sweeping, and caring for their families. The hospital is overpopulated with doctors and nurses. What is their other option for work?

The government here tells you where to live and can take your property at any time. The police don't seem fair and don't care if something is stolen.

The families in the hospital will break your heart. One family with their father, who was probably dying, touched my heart. The daughter had big tears in her eyes; you don't always see love like that. And that is huge with the Dominican people—the love they have for one another, not only for their families but for each other. The love is huge and extended to us daily. Americans can learn a lot about love for one another.

Americans have so much stuff, but do we always have love? Not just love for Christ but love for one another. In my own family, I know the answer is no, because most of my family members are self-serving and care only about their own feelings.

My little Berleny wanted to do crafts not only for herself but also for her sisters. My sister only thinks about herself and how things affect her. That's certainly not Christlike.

This trip was fourteen months in the making. I was honored I was asked to go in the midst of huge heartache. I was blessed to be a part of a team of women to love on these young girls and the family. I was blessed to sing "He's Got the Whole World in His Hands" in English, yet the motions to the song had no difference. The girls understood, the mothers even more, and on the last night, while singing, I looked at my leader with tears streaming down my face. Our eyes met, and our hearts knew what the other was thinking. Our lives have been blessed beyond measure. Our lives have been changed by crafts, songs, skits, and a lesson about God's love for us. It doesn't matter whether we are rich, poor, fat, thin, ugly, or beautiful; God loves us for us. He made us to show His love not just to those whose language we speak but to their hearts.

My life has been changed. A huge piece of my heart is staying in this country I may never see again. My heart has been turned upside down by the kids at the schools, hospitals, and churches we visited. My thoughts are full of the stories from each place, and I'll wonder daily how the people are. I'll picture their smiling faces every hour, and my heart will beat for them every minute.

I'm headed back to the United States now to see my family, to love on my animals, and to fall back into the routine of work and home. It's not easy to leave. I'll wonder every day if the people I encountered will think of me. If they do, I hope they know I'm thinking of them, praying them up, and loving them from here.

In the weeks since I've been home, I haven't shared my thoughts about this trip with very many people, mainly because no one has really asked. It's also not something I feel I should just say, "Hey, let me tell you about this trip I went on." That isn't really my personality. I've found my girls on Facebook, and I'm having fun talking to them. I'm learning more and more Spanish by talking to them, and I miss all of them. I especially miss the evening worship service with my husband and our evenings talking about the day. I miss the hourly focus on Christ and Christ alone. I miss the Dominican people and the teamwork they always display. Can Americans ever be this way?

I'm loving nine girls from afar and praying for them daily. I am waiting for God to answer a question: Should I go back to the DR? I'm also reminding my girls they are God's, I am God's, and we will someday be together again, always joined in this life by heart and spirit.

# December 31, 2016—What a Difference a Year Makes!

What a difference a year makes! This time last year, I was basking in the glow of celebrating my first New Year's with my then fiancé. I was hoping for that phone call from my daughter, and I was wishing my family would see they hurt people and then apologize for specific things that had transpired over the 2014–15 year.

Well, now I sit looking out my home office window and thinking about the past year. I was married in January 2016, and it was the one of the most wonderful days of my life. We had our closest friends and family there, minus my daughter, which was the only sadness to the day. My matron of honor, or best gal, as I prefer to call her, picked me up. We got our hair done, picked up lunch, and got ready together while watching the Hallmark Channel. When we were both dressed, we stepped out onto the balcony of our room and watched people come to the mansion, the snow making a fresh blanket in the sunlight.

The honeymoon in Colorado was awesome, and I enjoyed every moment of every day—fresh snow, the real fireplace, visiting the hot springs, the train ride to the top of a mountain with a picnic lunch in the snow, and lastly a beautiful sleigh ride to a cabin in the woods with dinner and another sleigh ride back to the car.

We celebrated Easter together, and one week later, the most amazing phone call from my daughter and her then fiancé. Fast-forward to one month later, and I'm watching my daughter come down a staircase and marry her guy with my husband performing the ceremony.

Fast-forward four more months, and we find out we are going to be grandparents. Our grandson should be here in late April, and I couldn't be more excited to step into this new role as Mimsy and Opa (personally, the names Grandma and Grandpa were ruined for me, so we looked for Scottish and German names for this honor).

Then, in July I took a trip to the beach with my best gal, and it was awesome. I didn't realize how tired I was, or emotionally spent, from the emotional roller coaster I had been on. We ate, slept, read, sat by the pool, floated in the pool, and watched the Hallmark Channel. My favorite part was our dinners and walks on the beach every night, talking about our families past, present, and future! I had never taken a trip with a friend, and we agreed this was a definite annual event. Our trip this year is in June!

Fast-forward to our mission trip to the Dominican Republic, and what a trip that was. My heart was not prepared for the whirlwind of emotions I would experience while on the trip and since.

Six weeks later, I left a job I'd had for eleven and a half years, and I've spent the past month sleeping, cleaning out closets, rearranging our home office, and taking care of me for a while.

Now, here I am looking back over this past year, and my heart feels like it could explode. I am blessed beyond belief with a husband, kids, three great friends, and a future grandson I cannot wait to meet! I watch my daughter and her pregnant belly, and she does things I did when I was pregnant. Her mannerisms are so me, and I can't help but smile that she is getting through her emotional roller coaster of past hurts and healing before her son gets here.

Although this year has been full of happiness and wonderful blessings, it's also been full of sadness at times. I recently talked to a friend and learned you can be full of joy but still be sad.

I'm sad at times because I see other women don't need or want good Christian friends like I do. I would love more women friends to talk about life with—what's going on in my marriage, with my kids, my family. When I was in a table group, it was so nice to talk about life and have others validate how I felt, or to question my motives. I see my daughter, and a friend's daughter, struggling with the same issues. I wonder why we aren't trying harder to bond.

I'm sad because I see my daughter and son-in-law struggling with issues I had as a young married person, and I wish I could solve their problems for them but know I can't. Their journey is their journey, but I can certainly be here to love, support, and listen.

I'm sad at times because sometimes I feel totally invisible to the universe. I've been gone from a volunteer program for three months, and only one person has called to ask if I was okay. No, I didn't leave the program to see whether anyone would call; I knew no one would. I left because I needed time to think, grow myself, and take a spiritual break. I just think it's weird you can be "so loved" and "needed," yet when you are gone, no one notices.

I took these issues a Christian sister, and we talked. I learned I'm not the only one who feels this way! So, if we are the church, and if we are to be the church, then why would people feel lonely?

At times, I think it's because people are so wrapped up in their own stuff that they do not take time to reach out. I know my own conscious is clear because I am a follow-upper! If I know you are hurt, scared, ill, down, or having a struggle, I follow up with you via text, call, or e-mail and make sure life is okay!

I know no two people are exactly alike, and I know I am more sensitive than most people. My friend told me I am "sensitive to the spirit," which makes me feel more deeply, and it was okay to question the who, what, why, and how of life.

I look to 2017 as a new opportunity waiting to grow me. I know I want to serve in different areas of church—ones that will grow me and give me an opportunity to meet new people and maybe make a new friend or two. My daughter, a mutual friend, and I are going to start a new adventure of attending a women's Bible study at church, and I'm excited about the people we may meet and the new friendships with which we may be blessed. I am excited about my first wedding anniversary with my dear, sweet husband who shows me every day what true, Godly love is all about! I am excited to meet my grandson in April or May, whenever He decides the little guy needs to arrive. I look forward to celebrating Mother's Day with my daughter, celebrating the first wedding anniversary of her and her husband in May, and my beach trip to relax, reflect, and renew!

I am ending this year by letting go of the hurts of 2016 and taking what I have learned about different personalities and the whys of others. I will use that knowledge to form new relationships!

I am ending this year by asking my Lord and Savior to lead me down the right path and be the wife, mother, and friend He calls me to be through His word and with His hands, guiding all I say and do.

I am ending this year being grateful and thankful to a Savior who unconditionally loves me with mercy and grace, and who always reaches His arms to me when I am sad or need a renewing of the spirit. I am ending this year thanking Him for the husband, kids, and friends I have in my life who show me love and compassion, rejoice in the good times, and give me support in the trying times.

I end this year being so full of love and blessings.

To my faithful WordPress readers and friends, I wish you all a blessed new year. Thank you for your words of encouragement.

Happy New Year in His love and grace.

# *Epilogue*

On April 7, 2016, my daughter called for the first time since our estrangement. I sat in my office at home watching my phone with her then fiancé's number lighting up. I called my husband at his Bible study and told him to come home. He rushed out of his men's group to receive the call with me. When we answered the phone, it was wonderful! I can remember hearing her voice and being so relieved. We had a good conversation, I thought, and we agreed to meet at a coffee shop. I remember telling her repeatedly, "I am sorry for everything that hurt you. I cannot change the past, but I can make our future better."

We met at the coffee shop, and I remember her husband (then fiancé) giving me a hug. I was so happy to have his arms around me. I had missed him also but missed my daughter more than words could say. I had a mixture of emotions between crying and wanting to laugh. She was able to meet my new husband, and he thought she was adorable!

The next few weeks were a mixture of joy and sadness. It seemed to me they were a mixture of trying to grow up and being extremely immature at the same time. They had so many issues to deal with at the moment, and it was difficult and stressful to keep up with all they were going through.

My husband became an ordained minister so he could perform their marriage ceremony. It wasn't an easy decision for him to make, but at the end of the day, he decided he would rather perform the wedding and have us both be a part of the day than not become a minister and have us not be included. The day was beautiful, but looking back on it, I wish I had just one photo of her and me at the wedding. The only pictures she was interested in were of her with her husband and with her friends. Each time I mentioned a photo of just her and me, I was told, "In a while." Needless to say, I was a little hurt, but we were still trying to repair our relationship, so I did not want to press the issue.

On their wedding night, they called us at about 9:15 p.m. and told us what they had been doing in the fancy hotel room, as well as what they had for dinner. They thanked us for their beautiful day. My daughter had been playing in the tub and was quite excited for the room and the entire experience of the hotel stay her former theater teacher had gifted them.

Three months after their wedding, they announced they were expecting their first child. That announcement brought more stress and drama than I could have ever imagined. One minute they were in love and going to last forever, and the next minute they wanted to divorce; he was leaving to never come back, thinking the baby and her would be better off without him. At one point, she was going to put the baby up for adoption, they were evicted from their apartment, and he lost his jobs and would be unemployed for two to three months at a time. During her pregnancy, her doctors thought her cancer was back due to extremely low iron, and she was referred to a hematologist and oncologist. She then began weekly doctor appointments, and I was happy I was able to take her to those appointments. In the meantime, my husband helped pay back payments of rent on their apartment, paid for their wedding and reception, gave them a down payment for their home, helped furnish their baby's room, gave them my car to drive for two years for free, bought her birthday presents from him, paid some medical bills because her husband never had health insurance for them, paid two years' worth of car insurance for them, bought groceries, paid some bills when they didn't have the money, bought him clothes and shoes to attend interviews and help get his photography business started, and bought groceries … only all to be kicked out of their lives again in March 2018.

Again, I felt it was all my fault and had done something so terrible that this situation could not be fixed. A whole new wave of depression, anxiety, and grief overcame my entire being. I had done everything God called me to do and provided all I felt God wanted us to provide. At first, I was angry at myself. Then I realized I was angry with God too. Why had He allowed this to happen again after I'd followed all He'd wanted to a *T*? It doesn't help when people talk about how this is her choice. I totally realize it is her choice, but that makes is harder, not easier.

Maybe part of Aurora doesn't want to face the fact she hurt her mom. Now that she's a mom, she sees how terrible it is to be away from a child, and she may not be able to face the fact her child may someday walk away from her. Studies have found that children who have parents who walk away from their parents are most likely to walk away too. Aurora's biological father hadn't spoken to his father or brothers in twenty-one years. Before that, his own father had disowned his brother (seventy years and counting). Even though I had nurtured Aurora for her entire life, nature is overpowering.

I should note here that my child and her husband do not have a relationship with his family either. Neither one of them has good, solid friendships, and neither has a good foundation for a "normal" parental relationship.

I totally take responsibility for the breakdown of communication between Aurora and me before our first estrangement. And over the past couple of years, while being in her life, I thought when she spoke to me about her marital or parenting issues, or when she spoke ill of her mother-in-law, she was just trying to get me to come to her side of argument. As a grown-up and a parent myself, I now see that you have to have both sides of a story at all times to make a sound decision. I don't know my son-in-law's parents, but I can speculate they tried their best as parents with what they had been given to deal with in life. They have two other grown children who are a big part of their lives. Sometimes parents make mistakes that cannot be taken back, and it's through our own spiritual and emotional maturity that we grow, learn, and process.

I've joined several online groups, and it is incredibly sad how many parents are without their children. I wonder what their story is, and when I see the parents who are estranged for ten, fifteen, or twenty years, it truly zaps any ounce of hope I have.

When she first left in 2018, I had to take down all her photos, packaged up all my grandson's toys and blankets, gave away his food I kept in my home, and cried for a month. Now, twenty-one months in, I'm beginning to get out photos and can talk about them with a lot of tears. I can think of the happy memories I have, but I do not pretend I will have them again. I could lie, and I could tell you I hold out hope I will see her, talk to her, hug her, and have a relationship again. But I will not allow myself to cling to that hope during this second estrangement. My hope at this point is the size of a mustard seed. But God tells me in Luke 17:6, "If you have faith as small as a mustard seed, you can say to this mulberry tree, 'be uprooted' and it will be obey you."

I remember her as she was, the last time I hugged her goodbye. She's my only child. There are moments I dream, and I want to pluck her from my dream and hug her for real. Then the alarm clock goes off, and I am snapped to a reality I don't want to live. I get up, get dressed, and go throughout my day hoping I don't run into anyone who asks me a question about my daughter and her family. I avoid church because I don't want the questions from the Bible study we attended regarding when we will return to the group. I avoid our local stores in the town close by for fear I will run into her, and she will turn and walk away like I've seen her do with other people she doesn't want to see.

She's not a monster, as she claims I am making her out to be. I will never say that about her, and I never have said anything remotely close. Yes, she has hurt me deeply, and it's a wound that never heals. She is lost, like most twentysomethings; she believes she know it all and that her way is the best way. For her spouse, I assume he thinks and feels the same. And anyone who voices an opinion or how they feel is narcissistic and wrong. According to her social media accounts, I am either a "worthless troll" or "narcissistic." All of these terms and comments should make me want to walk further away from her, but all it really does is make me wish someone would come along beside her, as people did for me, and walk her through her pain so she can reconcile our relationship.

My time with my grandson was incredibly precious to me. I loved cuddling him, changing his diaper, rocking him to sleep, and feeding him … the list goes on and on and on. The one thing about my daughter rejecting us again is our grandson has no clue who we are and why we are not there anymore. I can't imagine losing him when he could say our names, or have questions, or say, "I love you." I am thankful she chose to be estranged before this came to fruition.

The past two years with her were also very precious to me. I got to know her again and see how she was as a wife and mother. There were moments of her sleeping on my couch after each doctor visit, fixing her snacks, shopping with her, folding laundry … all these moments and conversations I adored, and no one can take the memory.

I got to know our son-in-law and his oddities and normalcies. He's adorable, and I truly hope he can always be himself. Standing next to him in church and hearing him sing as loud and as passionately as he did … those are memories no one can take.

No one can take away my mistakes either.

I married out of desperation at twenty-three. I wanted to experience life, and yes, that marriage was a mistake. Yes, I left him because he was a person with his own ghosts and demons to fight, and I was tired of him using me as the punching bag, emotionally and physically.

Yes, I married a second time to someone I truly thought I could make a life with. His mood swings, his hobbies, and his life were entirely different from mine, so our marriage fell apart almost as soon as it started. But he is someone who I still consider a friend today.

Yes, I asked an openly gay woman to move into my life and into my home after my second marriage fell apart. She was one of my best friends, and I thought I was learning about life and unconditional love from her, but I've learned through my groups at church only one person extends unconditional love to us, and that's God.

My daughter wanted me to confess to the world that our problems were totally my fault, and I was the only person to blame. I would jump through any hoop she threw at me, yet she has nothing but hate and disdain in her heart for me. She and her husband are the perfect people with the perfect life, and they make no mistakes and know how to handle every situation perfectly. I'm so happy for them— being in their early twenties and knowing it all! She can look into my life and tell me how I could have done it better, but she is not me, and she cannot understand what was in my mind when I made certain choices. Neither can she see my heart. From what she says and writes, she truly believes she and her husband can do parenting better than their parents and their grandparents. But let me point out their kids will have a very difficult time someday. Two perfect parents make for a very difficult upbringing and a lot of pressure for the children to live up to. The precedence has been set: "If you are not up to our standards, our beliefs, and our code, you too can be dismissed from our lives. We have done it to several people—what makes you think you're the exception?"

I look back over my daughter's childhood, and I see my mistakes clearly, but I also remember the times I would apologize for being grumpy or overreacting to situations.

Maybe I should have never answered the phone the first time she called.

Maybe I should have excused myself from her life.

I look back, and there are only a handful of times I can remember her extending an unsolicited "I love you." Her husband once told me she spent her entire life trying to fix me, and therefore she can't love me. Her hugs had no meaning and were simply a gesture she needed to extend because it was required, because I was hugging her.

She rarely extended a thank-you for things we did for them. She rarely remembered my birthday and certainly didn't celebrate Mother's Day with me. I'm not sure if I ever meant anything to her. I was simply a way of having free room and board, with meals cooked.

I have joined many Facebook groups for estranged parents, and every group and story is basically the same as what I've stated above. Parents are just a means to an end in some cases, and no real love is ever truly extended. We look at how our children treat others and wonder why we are not extended the same courtesies.

Looking back, I know there was a time my daughter loved me, and we had such good times. But about the time she was fourteen or fifteen, her entire personality changed. I knew I was the enemy, and no way would she ever extend grace and acceptance to me. Maybe that's why I continued to destroy myself in ways: no one on earth truly loved me, so what did it matter if I no longer existed? I had spent my entire life trying to be loved, and now my only child doesn't love me, so why do I matter?

If not for her leaving, however, I never would have immersed myself into church and searched for meaning. In a way, her leaving did help me find myself. I am a better wife, mother, daughter, friend, and person because I found myself. I always knew I was in here somewhere ... which is why I wrote this book.

As parents, we truly forget who we are and our purpose on earth. We let our roles define who we are. Whether my daughter realizes it or not, I threw myself into working and making money so she could enjoy her school years and not have to work while in high school. I guided her to adults who could help her fill out college applications, because I had no clue. I tried to teach her the value of a dollar by asking her to get a job and help pay her car insurance and half her car payment so maybe she would not wind up in her forties and working three jobs like I had to do. I was so focused on her life and helping her that I forgot to think of myself and what I may need to survive myself. All this cost me my relationship with her because I made mistakes, and she cannot and will not forgive me for them.

Because she wants me completely erased from her life, I wonder whether it will matter if I continue to recognize birthdays, anniversaries, and Christmases. I tried to take a hint from how she felt about her husband's family when they didn't reach out and was going to continue to reach out with cards and gifts. Then I realized, What's the point? There comes a time when you have to realize those who do not love you and do not want you in their lives want you to let them go. I can respect that wish, and slowly I am letting go.

It's not easy to not think of them. She is my first thought every morning and my last thought every night. I fall asleep praying for her. I dream of her. I have conversations in my head with her. There are days something happens, and my first thought is that I want to call her and laugh with her over it. There are days I want to talk to her husband and gain his perspective. There are days I want him to show me something on the computer or with my camera.

My therapist is teaching me to say, "I am okay even though my daughter is gone." The goal is to be able to say this without crying. After six months of practice, I can now say it without tears, but that doesn't make the pain less. I am discovering new hobbies and recently graduated from college with a degree in journalism. I am finding new direction in Bible study and trying to remember to stay connected to Christ so I can believe His truth and not the social media "hate my mom" frenzy.

Yet, I am hopelessly lost without her. I miss her every second of every day. At first, I grasped at straws, doing anything and everything I could to slowly get her back and to stay a part of her life. Over the past few months, she has made it crystal clear she wants nothing to do with me. She unfriended me on Facebook and Instagram, and then after three and a half months, her husband was also gone from these accounts, and I was blocked. No phone calls, no letters, no texts asking to work out our differences or problems. Again, I am left completely in the dark as to why all of the sudden I am a thing she can simply throw away. I can speculate and contemplate every single mistake I ever made, and all the things I wish I could do over, but God does not give us a do-over. He gives us a future to "go forward and sin no more," which is what I am doing now.

Most days, I feel completely alone. My husband doesn't understand because he has never had children of his own, yet he loved Aurora like she was his own. Her attack on him is devastating to me because he did absolutely nothing wrong; he loved her unconditionally, and that's it.

Her not speaking to my parents during this time is also heart-wrenching. I do not understand why she would shut them out. They love her and want what is best for her and her little family. Why she can't see love, I don't know.

Her two friends—one who used to be my neighbor—have distanced themselves from their own mothers. One friend is an alcoholic, and the other is addicted to prescription painkillers. Although I understand their distances, I am not sure why the one who claims to be a Christian would encourage Aurora to distance herself from me. I also don't understand completing cutting people out of your life, especially if you are a Christian, and God tells us to love everyone.

I still have issues with people saying, "God will take care of it," or, "This will resolve itself in God's timing," or, "This is Aurora's choice, so …" Nothing makes sense anymore, and I have a hard time thinking of what God's will for my life is during this time.

I am not sure of the lesson I am supposed to learn.

I am not sure what the plan for my life is anymore.

At times, I am not sure God hears my prayers. There was a period of time I could not even pray recently, but I told God I couldn't pray and to please just watch over every one of us because words seemed to be escaping me at this time.

I'm not sure why she insists on wanting to shame me on social media. Yes, I do check social media about once a week just to see if she is still alive—a practice I have learned all estranged parents do. We are not abnormal; we simply long for our children. She has bragged about reconnecting with her "stepmother," who was supposedly one of the reasons she left my home, yet now they are close. Nothing she does makes sense or moves toward resolving any issue we may have. I have learned all estranged children want their parents to be reduced to a pile of dust that can be easily swept away, or for our photos to be displayed on billboards for people to throw their rotten tomatoes at, as if this would make the estranged children somehow superior and reduce their pain to nothing.

I would love to be able to take any lashing she would wish to bestow upon me and for her hurt, anger, bitterness, and pain be gone magically. If she wants me to be reduced to tears, to hurt like she is hurting, she is getting her wish. But I know God has my hurt, and He wants our family to be reconciled. Aurora would tell you I am hiding my sins behind the curtain of religion, but the truth of the matter is when I asked God to forgive me for everything I had done wrong, for any heartache I had inflicted, He picked it up and carried it away. This is not for Aurora or me to do because God has already forgiven me. It is for Aurora and me to work through our issues and work together to build a better life. But until she is willing to do so, she will continue to hurt herself, her family, and our relationship. I cannot take away any of the hurt. I've tried, but she continues to hold tight.

Recently, my Bible online study group asked this question: "Where are you struggling with unbelief in your life right now?" This was my answer.

My daughter walked out of my life four years ago. She came back for two years, and then four months ago she walked out again. She assumes instead of talking things out. With the exit, I am no longer allowed to see my son-in-law or my grandson. She has also distanced herself from my parents, who are very hurt. I don't understand her thinking or her actions, and this time it took almost two months for me to even get out of bed and function. I prayed different prayers over the situation and finally told God I can't talk about her for the moment. I'm told that in the next life, I won't realize I'm not with her because in heaven, we won't have pain. There are days I want to be in heaven so I don't feel pain. I guess my relief from the unbelief is someday I'll be okay in this life without her. It is hard to think I'll be okay because my heart is missing pieces. But God will be with me every step of the way, He feels my pain, and He hurts when families are broken. So, God, hold my heart and my hurt and walk with me through my sorrow. Hold my child and her family and restore our relationship. Help me see the good work You are doing through the brokenness. In His name, I pray …

I blame myself daily and wonder whether the conversations I had with her husband about how to handle some of her moods is the cause of our estrangement. I wonder whether me telling other women our story when they tell me how nice it is that she and I are out doing things together and mention they haven't seen their own children because of estrangement is the cause. I wonder whether the fact that I speak to my parents and wanted her to so badly heal relationships with family is the cause. These are things I ponder daily.

In January 2019, we found out Aurora was going to be having a baby girl. In March, we learned she was born, and her name is Katherine, or Kate. Our grandson and granddaughter both have a plastic bin here at the house, and when I am out, if I see a gift I want to purchase for them, I buy it and put it in the bin. I also write to my grandchildren. Sometimes it is only one or two lines, and sometimes I write a funny story about Aurora that I remember. Sometimes I tell them I miss them and love them. One day, they will know my husband and I loved them, cherished them, and wished we could have been a part of their lives.

I wish I could end this book with a happy ending that gives you hope for your own estrangement. Just because my story didn't end with a complete restoration of the relationship, that doesn't mean yours won't. I pray for my life to be restored. I pray for the daughter I had in 2013 to return to me. I miss her in a way words cannot express. And every day that passes without being able to be a grandparent, a piece of me dies a little more.

If you are reading this book, and your story has ended as mine has for the moment, please know I am praying for you. I am praying for your child. God hears our prayers and feels the pain we feel. Surround yourself with people who build you up and can offer a shoulder to cry on, the people who will take you to lunch and laugh with your joys and cry with your sorrows. Being estranged from your child is grief that never ends. We have no closure and remain on edge, waiting for the next chapter to open and praying it ends different from the previous chapter. Being estranged creates a hole in your heart that stays open and empty. It creates holidays where something is always missing. It creates distance from other family members who want you, the parent, to remain the scapegoat or enemy. It creates sorrow to the very core of your being. I understand. I feel your pain. I carry your sorrow.

Aurora, as I sit on my couch watching the snowfall outside my window, the trees gently blow in the wind. I wish you here on my couch. We could chat about our children and the memories we have of them, both before and after estrangement, over a plate of slice-and-bake, gluten-free cookies and a cup of hot cocoa brimming with marshmallows. We would wallow in our self-doubt for a moment and remember all parents are imperfect people striving to do their best in a world of doubt. We would share our stories of heartbreak as we mourn for our children and discuss what holidays, birthdays, and other celebrations are like with the one missing piece of our hearts. We would talk until our thoughts were expelled and our eyes were red and swollen from the tears we have cried not only today but every time we talk about our missing piece. We would sigh, take one last drink of our cocoa, and realize the afternoon was gone and it was time to part ways. But before we go, I would squeeze your hand one last time, brush the tear from your cheek, and remind you that you are not alone. God is with you. My heart is with you. Our journey is far from over. As you move forward, you'll remember this day, and when you feel you are drowning in sorrow, you'll remember others are out there who share your pain.

> Consider it pure joy, my brothers and sisters, whenever you face trials of many kinds, because you know that the testing of your faith produces perseverance. Let perseverance finish its work so that you may be mature and complete, not lacking anything. (James 1:2–4 NIV)

# *Resources*

Support Group for Parents on Facebook I have found helpful: "Parents Grieving for Living Children; Estranged Parents and Grandparents"

Books I have read that helped with the pain:

McGregor, Sherri. *Done with the Crying: Help and Healing for Mothers of Estranged Children*, Sowing Creek Press, May 2, 2016

TerKeurst, Lysa. *It's Not Supposed to Be This Way*, Thomas Nelson Publishing, November 13, 2018